NO BAD HIRES

BAD HIRES ARE NOW OPTIONAL

To Peyton,
With thanks for your
support and encouragement

Chuck Russell

Chuck Russell

Published by Johnson & James

Printed in the United States of America

Russell, Chuck

    No Bad Hires

    (Bad Hires Are Now Optional)

Library of Congress Catalog Card Number

ISBN - 9781708719715

DEDICATION

To my wonderful wife, Lauretta, whose love helped me through the economic rollercoaster ride of entrepreneurial bootstrapping.

To my daughter, Lacey, and my son, Jamey, who made it all fun.

To Robert White, my partner, who built the amazing IT system that made my ideas come to life.

To Dr. Leonard Goodstein, Dr. Stephen Brand and Dr. Paul Barrett, who had all the credentials and special education yet still listened to me and my disruptive ideas.

PURPOSE

The purpose of this book is to answer the questions that you have always had about hiring the right people for the right jobs. It is not an idea or a clever concept. It is a simple, practical way to fundamentally avoid bad hires. You can put it to use right away after reading the book. It could be that you already made your last bad hire.

The BestWork DATA Mission Statement

To touch the lives of hundreds of millions of people so that they can see themselves through their strengths and not their weaknesses and so that they better understand other people.

Our products must:

- Honor each person.
- Offer a positive emotional experience.
- Provide actionable information.

TABLE OF CONTENTS

Have you ever hired anyone whose performance was not what you expected?

Would you like to know why that is happening and if it will ever change?

THEN THIS IS THE BOOK

YOU HAVE ALWAYS WANTED TO FIND.

BAD HIRES ARE NOW OPTIONAL

THE KEY
TO SUCCESS
AND
PROFITABILITY
IN BUSINESS
IS HAVING
THE RIGHT
PEOPLE
IN THE RIGHT
JOBS.

The Hard Facts

Hiring in most companies is broken. Employees are hired of course, but rarely do the companies get the performance they wanted. An extensive three-year study[1] of more than 5,000 hiring managers revealed that only 19% of new hires went on to be successful in the opinion of the hiring companies. The 81% of unsuccessful hires included:

- Candidates with superb technical skills and knowledge.
- Candidates who were successful in other companies.
- Candidates who interviewed beautifully, on video in some cases.
- Candidates with stunning resumés.
- Candidates who seemed to match the culture of the company.
- Candidates with highly respected educations.
- Candidates that matched profiles created by some assessment.

These unsuccessful employees are being hired by intelligent people, using the best methods they could find. Sadly, many companies have adapted their decision making and their expectations to fit these incredibly low results. It does not have to be that way. If so many people are successful only one out of five times, there is a fundamental flaw in understanding the problem.

---

[1] Leadership IQ's Global Talent Management Survey, 2012.

THE BEST IDEAS

OFTEN FAIL

WITHOUT THE RIGHT PEOPLE

IN THE RIGHT JOBS.

A Far, Far Better Way

The key to success and profitability in business is having the right people in the right jobs. The best ideas often fail without the right people in the right jobs. Countless books have been written, an endless array of seminars have been held, and an army of experts have offered their solutions on how to get those right people into the right jobs. Billions of dollars have been spent, billions of hours have been used, and…it has gotten a little bit better. Of course, the fast-casual food business has a turnover rate of over 100%. Many call centers aspire to have that rate. Sales forces routinely expect a third or more of their salespeople to produce little or nothing. This is "explained" by the Pareto Principle or the 80/20 Rule. What if that is wrong? What if the actual reason is simply people are in the wrong jobs? What if that was easy to fix? Ideas and assessments that make it "a little bit better" are clearly not enough. In a world of technology, with science making quantum leaps almost daily, there is now a far, "better" way…a

4

disruptive innovation that radically changes the way we understand talent acquisition and talent management. That disruptive innovation is BestWork DATA.

That is exactly what this book is about. It is about a simple solution to what has previously been a complex problem. With that DATA, fast-casual food stores leading the industry with an 86% turnover reduced that to 52%. A pest control company with an over 100% turnover of technicians began using DATA to both hire and manage the technicians. Within three years, the turnover dropped to 10%. These results are not just *better*. They are **game changing.**

> **IMPORTANT NOTE:** At this point, some readers are fully engaged and cannot wait to get to the *How Do I Do It* part. For you, continue on right here. Some other readers are incredulous and cannot wait to get to the *How is That Possible* part. For you, take a slight detour to the Chapter 15 and read *What Changed*. After that, you will be ready for the *How Do I Do It* part.

Today, Bad Hires Are Optional

Imagine…you get to decide how many Bad Hires you want to make. Just like the gas pedal on your car, if you want to accelerate the growth and profitability of your company, simply reduce, or even eliminate Bad Hires completely. If your company's growth is out of control, add a few Bad Hires and Presto! Growth will slow down or even come to a halt. Of course, that is ridiculous. No business wants Bad Hires. **Even job seekers don't want to be Bad Hires.** That can quickly turn them from employees back into job seekers.

So, how is this No Bad Hires thing possible? Remember that one day you were writing down directions and looking at road maps, and then GPS appeared. No more writing down directions…No more road maps…And most amazing, no more *getting lost* at all. The very concept of getting lost vanished. As long as you had the address, the app would get you there. GPS was not just *better* than road maps and directions. It was a whole new world. In a digital world, science takes quantum leaps. It goes from *better* to *whole new world* faster than you can imagine, opening up extraordinary opportunities and possibilities that seemed impossible only a short time ago. In the one or two hours it will take you to read this book, your business world will never be the same. You will have opened the door into a universe of human potential that will ultimately transform virtually every aspect of human experience and interaction.

EVEN JOB SEEKERS DON'T WANT TO BE BAD HIRES.

CHAPTER 1

WHAT IS A BAD HIRE?

A Bad Hire is a smart, hard-working person who lacks the hard-wired traits and cognitive abilities needed to deliver the behaviors that are necessary to succeed in the job.

What Is a Bad Hire?

The obvious answer is someone who does not do the job. It can be the salesperson who does not make sales. It can be the manager who does not manage. It can be the retail store associate who does not greet customers. It can be a thousand versions of this, but to stop hiring Bad Hires, you need a better definition and a better understanding of exactly what is keeping that person from doing the job.

The Really Bad Hire

First, there are two clear types of Bad Hires. The best Bad Hire is really awful. Everyone can see that they are a Really Bad Hire.

They are lazy.

They have a bad attitude.

They don't do the work.

They don't listen.

They blame other employees.

They have a million excuses for why nothing is getting done. Everyone can see these things. Nothing positive is happening. This type of Bad Hire is usually dismissed in a relatively short period of time. It is the least expensive type of Bad Hire. They cost the least money, time and energy. Fortunately, these Bad Hires are relatively rare.

Close…But Still a Bad Hire

The second type of Bad Hire is by far the worst, the most costly and easily, the most frustrating: they can **almost** do the job. Some examples of this are:

> That salesperson has a lot of activity…*and there are some deals in the works*. We've spent a lot of time with them, working on their presentation…*and it's getting better all the time*. Yes, they have been here for a year or so…*but if just one or two of these deals close…*

> They were promoted to management last year…*but we were so busy, they didn't really have time to learn the new job that well*. I really haven't had that much time to work with them…*but I think things are freeing up now, so with my help…* Now that they have gone through that management training program…*I expect they will know how to take charge of their team*. It takes time to learn the ins and outs of management anyway…

> They have the project manager certification… *that means they know how to do this stuff, right?* Maybe, it's just a matter of experience. Once they've been here… *That long! Already?* Is there some course we can send them to? Maybe a coach or consultant? … *We've got a lot of money invested in them. This needs to work.*

THE SECOND TYPE

OF BAD HIRE

IS BY FAR THE WORST,

THE MOST COSTLY

AND EASILY,

THE MOST FRUSTRATING:

THEY CAN ALMOST DO THE JOB.

Every business in the world has found itself with some employee that could **almost** do the job. That employee was likable, easy to coach, hard-working and close to succeeding. They just needed more (pick one):

- Time
- Training
- Coaching
- Mentoring
- Luck

Yet, whatever was added, it was never enough for them to achieve success. Situations like this can sometimes resemble a swim team with the coach working hard to keep his swimmers from drowning. While he is occasionally successful with this rescue operation, the original goal of the team was to win swim meets.

The Wrong Equation

This is the equation that such admirable efforts are based upon.

$$\textbf{Ability + Training + Experience + Motivation = Job Success}$$

Once the person is hired, it is assumed that their **ability** to do the job is adequate. Then **training** & **motivation** become the primary means of influencing job performance. **Experience** grows with time. But, what if that first assumption is wrong? What if their ability to do the job is not adequate? What if you are training and motivating a person four feet tall to slam dunk basketballs? The concept is exciting for both of you. The training is certainly engaging. The problem is that the rim of the basket is just too high. All the training and all the motivation is never going to enable that four foot tall player to slam dunk the ball without a ladder or trampoline. In other words, it would require a dramatic change in the game itself for it to work.

Hidden Bad Hires

Have you ever been to a restaurant where the food was good, the ambience was pleasing and the service was efficient but impersonal?

The experience was acceptable but not exceptional. The waitstaff did almost what was expected of them. The only part that was missing was the warm and friendly connection that makes the meal special. It is unlikely that you would revisit this restaurant. If you related the story of your experience to others, it is unlikely they would choose to try the restaurant. This is an example of a Hidden Bad Hire. The owner sees good food being served efficiently. There are no complaints. Yet the Hidden Bad Hire has cost the restaurant multiple future customers.

HIDDEN BAD HIRES ARE A FAR GREATER PROBLEM THAN THE OBVIOUS BAD HIRES.

In a competitive market, Hidden Bad Hires make the difference between success and failure…the retail associate who doesn't greet customers, the customer service agent who lacks empathy, the supervisor who doesn't enforce the safety rules, the sales rep who doesn't quite qualify the prospect, the project manager who misses details and the manager who gives fuzzy feedback to the employees. All of these Hidden Bad Hires erode the profitability and goodwill of the enterprise.

Some managers may even be reluctant to get rid of Hidden Bad Hires. They may have become comfortable in handling the performance issues. They may have made concessions to accommodate the subpar performance. Even if they did remove the Hidden Bad Hire, there is no guarantee that the next person will be better.

The effect of Hidden Bad Hires is amplified in small businesses and within small workgroups. If a business has 10% of its people in the wrong jobs, it will struggle. **If 20% of its people are in the wrong jobs, it will struggle to be profitable.** If more than that, it will struggle to survive. In large companies and within large workgroups, the effect is substantial, but the Hidden Bad Hires often become lost in the crowd. It is not uncommon for one third of a salesforce to be incapable of executing the necessary sales strategy. As with other examples of Hidden Bad Hires, the performance gap is explained by a lack of training or experience. Consequently, huge sums of money are then spent attempting to solve the problem by training the right skills with the wrong people.

A BETTER DEFINITON OF A BAD HIRE

A Bad Hire is a smart, hard-working person who lacks the hard-wired traits and cognitive abilities needed to deliver the behaviors that are necessary to succeed in a particular job.

This definition shatters every paradigm about hiring, training and managing. It fills in the missing pieces to thousands of really interesting but less than effective ideas on performance management. It is the key to getting *the right people into the right jobs[2]*. It is the key to *getting the wrong people off the bus and the right people on the bus.[3]* It explains why some salespeople never found the *solution to selling solutions,[4]* failed to embrace the *Challenger Sale[5]*, and why other salespeople never got the *spin[6]* just right on their selling. It is why some managers could *manage in one minute,[7]* and other managers never seemed to find the time. It is why some never could find that darn *cheese[8]*. There have been countless models attempting to explain job performance. The implication is always that if the models are clearly understood, then successful performance can be coaxed from virtually anyone with enough training. This is not true, but it can provide a remarkably entertaining and expensive consulting and training project with fascinating discussions. **The inescapable fact is that if an individual lacks the critical strengths and abilities necessary to deliver the job behaviors for a particular position, they will never be able to excel, and they will struggle to achieve even adequate performance.**

---

[2] Chuck Russell, <u>Right Person - Right Job, Guess or Know</u> (Johnson & James, 1996).
[3] Jim Collins, <u>Good To Great</u> (HarperCollins, 2001).
[4] Michael Bosworth, <u>Solution Selling</u> (McGraw Hill, 1995).
[5] Matthew Dixon & Brent Adamson, <u>The Challenger Sale</u> (Penguin, 2011).
[6] Neil Rackham, <u>Spin Selling</u> (McGraw Hill, 1988).
[7] Ken Blanchard & Spencer Johnson, <u>The One Minute Manager</u> (William Morrow Company, 1986)
[8] Spencer Johnson, <u>Who Moved My Cheese</u> (G.P. Putnam's Sons, 1998).

It is important to remember that everyone is a Bad Hire for some jobs. In fact, most Bad Hires are good people in the wrong jobs. Some Bad Hires were actually good hires until their job changed, and their strengths no longer matched the ones needed for the new job.

- No one is a good hire for all jobs.
- All companies want the right people in the right jobs.
- Job seekers want to be in the right job.
- The company hired a Bad Hire because it looked like a good hire.
- The job seeker took the wrong job because it looked like the right one.

The problem is that everyone is operating with poor or incomplete information. Today, with BestWork DATA, that is no longer necessary.

> **NOTE:** In this book, DATA, with all capital letters, refers to BestWork DATA's measurement of an individual's hard-wired personality traits and cognitive abilities.

NO ONE

IS A GOOD HIRE

FOR ALL JOBS.

MOST BAD HIRES

ARE GOOD PEOPLE

IN THE WRONG JOBS.

CHAPTER 2

A PRACTICAL MODEL
OF JOB PERFORMANCE

For every type of job, there are a few critical factors that are absolutely necessary in order to be successful at that particular job.

The Traditional Model of Job Performance

Job performance has traditionally been understood through a two-part model (Illustration A). One part consists of the intangible factors such as Motivation, Attitude, Values, Work Ethic and Interests. The other part consists of Skills, Experience and Education.

Illustration A. Traditional Model of Job Performance

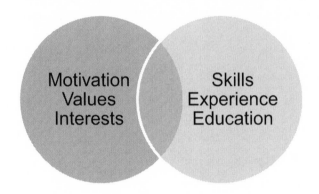

With this model of understanding, if an employee was motivated and had a good attitude, it made sense that their job performance could be increased with training and experience. The more they learned about the job, the better they could do the job. Many times, this was exactly what happened. Unfortunately, many times it did not. Despite expensive and widely acclaimed training programs delivered by skilled trainers, the performance of certain employees just never seemed to improve to any significant degree. New employees were said to be in a *learning curve*. Once they gained enough experience, their performance was sure to improve. Again, this was true for many of them, but some never seemed to come out of that *learning curve.*

If an employee had the skills and experience to do the job but still was not performing the job adequately, it was assumed to be a motivation problem. With strong motivation, performance was sure to happen. Sometimes positive motivation was used.

Reach this goal and you get a bonus!

Sometimes negative motivation was used.

If you do not reach this goal, you're fired.

Sometimes the motivation worked; performance improved and all was well. Unfortunately, at other times, job performance was still unsatisfactory. At these times, positive motivation was sometimes changed to negative motivation or vice versa. Still, nothing really changed the job performance.

The Missing Piece of the Puzzle

There was a piece of the puzzle missing from the model. With only part of the model, it was not surprising that it only worked part of the time. In the early 1990's, for the first time, serious psychometric assessment instruments were developed specifically to correlate hard-wired personality traits and cognitive abilities with job performance. These instruments used the latest psychological models of personality and the latest thinking on cognition. They also used more effective formats in their questionnaires. The most important point, however, was that now they were measuring hard-wired traits and abilities. These performance factors did not change with training, coaching or incentives. When this data was added to the traditional model, as seen below in Illustration B, it shattered the old paradigms of performance management. If an individual lacked the critical strengths needed for a particular job, no amount of training was going to raise their performance to an acceptable level. No amount of experience could give them those strengths. No amount of motivation could make up for that lack.

Illustration B. 90's Understanding of Job Performance

Cognitive Abilities & Personality Traits

Motivation Values Interests

Skills Experience Education

IMPORTANT NOTE: Simple personality surveys had been sold in the business world for decades. Adjective checklists were the earliest form of these. They were soon followed by products such as DISC and Myers-Briggs, all of which were meant to be simple counseling tools in the early part of the last century. While these early assessments offered fun insights and made for interesting discussions, the information they provided lacked the accuracy and reliability for serious business decisions. To be sure, using them did bring additional information for hiring decisions and that was often an improvement over using no assessments at all. However, it was not until the 90's that truly accurate and reliable instruments were available, and the information they provided was far superior to the simpler tools. To learn more, visit www.aboutassessments.com.

IF AN INDIVIDUAL

LACKS THE CRITICAL STRENGTHS

NEEDED FOR A PARTICULAR JOB,

NO AMOUNT OF TRAINING

IS GOING TO RAISE

THEIR PERFORMANCE

TO AN ACCEPTABLE LEVEL.

"Short" Doesn't Change Either

A fun way to visualize how the three circles work is to imagine an athlete who dreams of being a professional basketball player in the NBA. They are passionate and highly motivated. They are willing to practice and train for long hours, even beyond what most other players are willing to do. They listen to the coach, and do their very best to follow those instructions. They definitely **want to play professional basketball.**

They are fast, with quick hands and exceptional agility. They have played basketball for all of their years in school. They know how to dribble the ball and shoot baskets. They **know how to play.**

They are short. They are still motivated and they still know how to play, but on an NBA basketball court, they will live in a world of armpits and elbows. The average NBA player is taller with a far greater reach. The other players in the NBA are just as quick and have pretty much the same skills. They are also motivated and determined to work hard. Just like hard-wired personality traits and cognitive abilities, "**short**" does not change. The shorter they are, the more extra effort and energy it will take to simply stay on the court with the taller players. It will be almost impossible for them to excel in basketball.

Example: Spud & Muggsy

What about Spud Webb and Muggsy Bogues? Famous NBA players? Spud was 5'7"; Muggsy was 5'3". Both were exceptional athletes, with exceptional skills driven by extraordinary determination. They both had careers in professional basketball despite being short. Crowds came to see them compete in a world of giants. They were not top scorers and their defensive play was not outstanding. If both had been on the same team, it would be hard to imagine that team winning. Despite their accomplishments, no NBA team scouts for short players. Similarly, businesses do not want their strategies to be built on finding amazing exceptions like Spud and Muggsy. BestWork DATA gives them the ability to pursue a more predictable path to success.

What Difference Does It Make in Business?

The advent of these new instruments in the 90's opened the door to a world of research in hundreds of companies of all types. The findings were astounding. A key study of 200 companies across a variety of industries and jobs demonstrated the remarkable possibilities of these tools. When the hard-wired personality traits and cognitive abilities of the employees were matched to the job behaviors needed to perform a specific job, the **average** increase in job performance was 25%. The increase was even higher on average with jobs that primarily required knowledge work. The missing part of the job performance model had been found.

Since that time, the tools for reliably measuring those factors have been dramatically improved. What used to require an hour or more, now can be done in 25 minutes, and with greater accuracy. Cognitive measurement is now known to be vital to understanding job performance in every type of job. It turns out that all people are "smart" but in different ways, and some ways are best for some jobs but not for others. Without cognitive information, it is impossible to know whether the person can handle the extended routine of some jobs or the complex product knowledge of other jobs. It is critical to understanding the communication issues that occur between people. School grades and college degrees of any kind are not reliable indicators of cognitive ability. It requires a sophisticated instrument designed for that purpose.

WHEN THE HARD-WIRED
PERSONALITY TRAITS AND
COGNITIVE ABILITIES OF THE
EMPLOYEES WERE MATCHED
TO THE JOB BEHAVIORS
NEEDED TO PERFORM
A SPECIFIC JOB,
THE <u>AVERAGE</u> INCREASE
IN JOB PERFORMANCE
WAS 25%.

It was not just the addition of cognitive data that caused the dramatic leap in the efficacy of testing. Psychologists had finally mapped out a structure of personality traits, called the Big Five[9] after the five major factors in the model. Extensive research had proven these factors to be invaluable in understanding human behavior, as they defined the hard-wired elements of personality. They could be counted on to remain stable and therefore they could be used to make predictive decisions, unlike DISC and Myers-Briggs models which reported on *states* rather than *traits. States* tended to change depending upon mood, circumstances or other variables. This made for chancy decision-making that seemed to work one time but not the next. For these reasons, these must never be used for hiring decisions. The measurement of hard-wired personality traits has replaced simple DISC-based quadrant models. Such models, along with Myers-Briggs, have long been entertaining introductions to personality differences. Just as X-rays have given way to CAT scans and MRI's that provide deeper data, enabling more accurate diagnoses for physicians, more advanced psychometric instruments, such as BestWork DATA, are enabling more effective hiring decisions for businesses. More information on the qualitative differences of assessment products is available at www.aboutassessments.com.

---

[9] Robert R. McCrae and Paul T. Costa. "Validation of the Five-Factor Model of Personality Across Instruments and Observers." Journal of Personality and Social Psychology, 1987, Vol. 52, No. 1.

WITHOUT COGNITIVE
INFORMATION,
IT IS IMPOSSIBLE
TO KNOW WHETHER
THE PERSON CAN HANDLE
THE EXTENDED ROUTINE
OF SOME JOBS
OR THE COMPLEX
PRODUCT KNOWLEDGE
OF OTHER JOBS.

A More Practical Model of Job Performance

The new model made sense but how did the pieces fit together? Which one was more important? What does this change? The answer to that question was **EVERYTHING**. Talent acquisition and talent management would never be the same again. In fact, the world of training and consulting would never be the same. More about this later.

First, it is important to understand the model, and that is best done with some more descriptive or behavioral terminology (see Illustration C).

Illustration C. The New Model of Job Performance

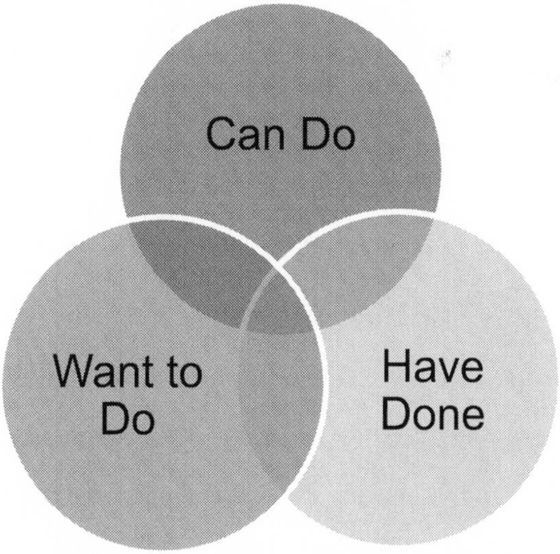

The intangibles of *motivation, attitude, values, work ethic* and *interests* essentially indicate what the individual ***wants to do***. That can change over time and with circumstances. It can be influenced by many things. It is an important contributor to job performance, and should always be considered, but it is not a reliable predictor of that job performance. In fact, if you motivate people who are in the wrong jobs, they just make mistakes faster.

An individual's *skills, education and experience* tell **what they know** and **what they have done**. It is important to consider these things, but effective training can enhance *skills* and *job knowledge*, and *experience* will grow over time. People can always learn more. The fact that someone has the skills and experience in the job does not ensure that they can or will deliver the job performance needed in another situation. The management can be different. The work environment can be different. The competitive market can require different strategies. Success in another company, even in the same job, is not a reliable predictor of job performance in another company.

Personality traits, as measured with current technology, **do not change** appreciably over time or with training or coaching. The same is true of *cognitive abilities*. This stability is incredibly important. It means that a person's strengths are reliable. They can be depended on to act the same way under the same circumstances. Therefore, measuring *personality traits* and *cognitive abilities* shows **what they can do**. When this is related to the job behaviors that are necessary for satisfactory job performance, it is a reliable predictor of that job performance.

IF YOU MOTIVATE PEOPLE
WHO ARE IN THE WRONG JOB,
THEY JUST MAKE MISTAKES FASTER.

The Wrong Road of Profiling

How was this **can do** information used with other information to make hiring decisions? Employers wanted to hire a person just like the person who was their top performer. It seemed to make sense to test top performers, and then to use those measurements to create a *profile* or *template for success*. That *profile* or *template* could then be used to compare job candidates to see which ones were most like the top performers. Various methods of calculating the degree to which a candidate matched the *profile* were used. These generated a percentage which indicated how closely the candidate matched the *profile*. Generally, a percentage match of 70% was considered to be acceptable. A match of 80% was considered to be good, and anyone with a matching percentage over 90% should be hired immediately. This methodology seemed to be logical and it should work. Only it didn't...not as well as expected. Experience revealed two major problems:

1. Who is a *Top Performer*?

At first, the answer seems easy. For a sales team, it must be the person who sells the most. Or is it the person whose sales are the most profitable? Or perhaps, it is the person who sells the right products or services? At times, clients named the new salesperson, who really had not sold anything to speak of, but who everyone felt was going to be a star. Other "ringers" were the salesperson of record for huge customers that they successfully serviced, but which they had not sold. It was the rare customer who had solid objective data that described a "top performer" profile, and with which everyone agreed. Statistical validity was another problem. Sample sizes with only a few members were questionable at best.

2. What Is Missing?

Selecting a parachute is a good metaphor for hiring. Picking out a wonderful color combination is **nice**. Having a comfortable harness with easily-adjustable straps is **important**. Having a parachute that opens successfully every time is **critical.** Similarly, a candidate who possesses all of the **nice** and **important** factors for a particular job but who lacks one or more of the **critical factors** for that job is a **Bad Hire**, regardless of the percentage matching score.

Profiling methodologies combine all of the factors measured into a single percentage indicating the degree to which the candidate matched the profile on all factors. Some systems allowed users to adjust the importance of certain factors, but still produced a single percentage score. This is the fatal flaw in the profiling concept. All factors do not contribute equally, and even upgrading the importance of some is no more than guesswork. Even after doing that, the factors are still stirred together in one pot to make that particular "hiring stew". The reality is that for every type of job there are a few **critical factors** that are absolutely necessary in order to be successful at that particular job.

> **Example:** A company was hiring salespeople for a persuasive sales position. They had created a profile using top performers. This was actually done with fairly strong data and a meaningful sample size. Candidate A's test results showed a 92% match to the profile of top performers. The client's reaction: "Wow! Don't let them leave the building. Hire them right away!" Fortunately, a consultant who was familiar with that assessment, examined the raw data. It turned out that the missing 8% was the ability to close sales or to persuade prospects to make buying decisions. In other words, it was a beautiful parachute, and it was marvelously comfortable, but it wouldn't open.

Unfortunately the world of assessment profiling is full of such examples. There are advantages when the profiles are rigorously developed with strong statistical sample and objective metrics. There will still be some parachutes that partially open or as in the example, do not open at all. Too many profiles are sold without the rigor, without solid statistical samples and without reliable metrics.

THE REALITY IS

THAT FOR EVERY TYPE OF JOB

THERE ARE A FEW

CRITICAL FACTORS

THAT ARE ABSOULTELY NECESSARY

IN ORDER TO BE SUCCESSFUL

AT THAT PARTICULAR JOB.

Bundled Information Can Be Misleading

Even when profiles were done correctly, hiring decisions suffered from an unintended consequence of the three circle model (see Illustration D). The original model with the three circles presented each of the three elements as being part of the hiring decision.

Illustration D. Traditional Hiring Decision Factors

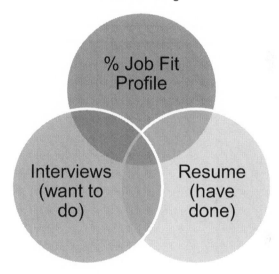

The information seemed to be of equal importance even though the reliability of each one often varied considerably. The **can do** part was usually presented as a percentage match to a profile, and this was called *job fit*. This was usually accompanied by a summary with the various elements bundled up into a generalized report. Interviews varied according to the skill and experience of the interviewers. Resumés and references varied according to the skill of the writers. Hiring decisions tended to average all of these together. An outstanding resumé or a terrific interview could boost a mediocre job fit into a positive hiring decision. Conversely, many companies were overwhelmed by hundreds of resumés, all sounding alike. Interviews frequently seemed inconclusive. Looking for something on which to base a decision, they defaulted to the job fit percentage score, believing that to be a confirmation of a good hire. Even though the hiring model included all three circles, actual practice was quite different. Sound hiring decisions were still elusive and **Bad Hires** still happened.

CHAPTER 3

JOB BEHAVIORS...

NOT JOB DESCRIPTIONS

Most often, job descriptions are bloated laundry lists that confuse instead of clarifying the picture of the ideal candidate.

Burn the Job Descriptions

One of the major obstacles to hiring effectively is, ironically, the job description. Rather than being a careful and specific set of the key components of the job, job descriptions are most often bloated laundry lists that confuse instead of clarifying the picture of the ideal candidate. Not wanting to omit anything that might be relevant to the job, all manner of things are included. Part of this is driven by legal fears within larger companies. In trying to avoid ever requiring an employee to do something beyond the requirements of their job, everything that can be included is included.

> **Baffling Example:** A group of managers at a large company was shown nine different job descriptions with the job titles removed. All of the jobs were within the work teams of the managers, but no one could match the job titles with the job descriptions. Imagine a job seeker's confusion with such descriptions.

The information that is most commonly used to match to such job descriptions is the resumé. How are resumés written? Job seekers want to include anything and everything that might possibly make a connection with one of those wide-ranging job postings. Consequently, any definition of the candidate's real capabilities is often lost among the clutter. Along with this, professional resumé writers, career coaches and the host of online services have ensured that poor resumés are rare.

So, the challenge for recruiters is to match inflated resumés with bloated job descriptions. Yet, inside every resumé is a good hire for some jobs and a bad hire for other jobs. Inside every job description is a good job looking for the right hire. Now, there is a simpler and more effective way of matching talent to jobs.

Renting Job Behaviors

The true objective of hiring any employee is to rent *job behaviors*. These are the behaviors that the company needs to operate successfully. For example:

- Directing the actions of other employees
- Persuading prospects to make buying decisions
- Accurately handling highly detailed information
- Performing effectively in stressful situations
- Projecting warmth and friendliness to customers
- Complying with established rules and procedures
- Performing a routine set of tasks on a daily basis
- Solving unexpected problems
- Delivering creative and innovative solutions
- Reacting to unexpected events (walk up customers)

Each of these is a specific *job behavior* that the business needs to operate successfully. If the employee fits the success profile, but does not persuade prospects to make buying decisions, it is a **Bad Hire**. If the person interviews with energy and enthusiasm, but cannot deliver that same energy and enthusiasm on a daily basis with customers, it is a **Bad Hire**. Would it make sense to make sure that the job candidate can deliver the necessary *job behaviors* before hiring them?

Sports follows this principle. Ideally, the baseball team wants a player who hits .300 and is a wonderful teammate. They will take a player who is hitting .300 but is not a wonderful teammate in the clubhouse. They do not want and have no interest in a wonderful teammate whose average is .150. Sports does an excellent job of separating the necessary *job behaviors* from the *nice to have* characteristics.

Today, technology enables companies to easily verify the job candidates' ability to deliver specific *job behaviors*. All *job behaviors* depend upon certain hard-wired traits and abilities. These are quickly measured in BestWork DATA's 25-minute online survey and are translated into easily understood descriptions of each individual's ability to deliver the necessary *job behaviors*. If they cannot, they can be exited from the selection process. If they can, then it makes sense to explore their skills, knowledge, experience, values, cultural fit and other elements. This focus on *job behaviors* dramatically reduces Bad Hires, even making them optional.

When Screening & Selection Are Mixed

There are two very different objectives within every effective hiring process:

- Screening out candidates that cannot do the job in question
- Selecting the best candidate from the ones that remain

Most companies combine these. A pool of job candidates is acquired, and in a digital world, that can mean hundreds of applications. A common filtering step is to pick out one or two easily identified facts that appear on the resumés, and then to use those facts as sorting points. Examples:

- Years of experience
- Specific types of experience
- Level of education
- A specific degree
- Certification
- Titles of former jobs

While these may be relevant information, there is rarely a direct connection with actual job performance. A world of exceptions exists, and many of the exceptions became outstanding performers. Many of candidates that pass through this screen ultimately fail. The reason facts such as these are used is that they can be used. These facts can be identified, while the rest of most selection processes becomes a world of interviews and discussions in which subjectivity rather than objectivity reigns.

Screening out candidates with these types of resumé facts can cripple a company's talent acquisition. In a competitive talent market, such common factors narrow the scope of recruiting. One highly successful client had a dozen openings unfilled throughout the year in a job that paid extremely well with full benefits. They were screening out any candidates who lacked five years of specialized experience in a relatively narrow industry. There just were not that many of those left in the talent market. When the primary focus shifted to looking for the right job behaviors, the client discovered that the right job candidates, with the Critical job behaviors, could be trained and taught the necessary product knowledge. Experience would follow. The set number of years of experience was removed as a job requirement. It was still considered an advantage if a candidate had it, but no longer were candidates disqualified for lacking it. This change opened up entirely new sources of talent.

SCREENING OUT CANDIDATES USING RESUMÉ FACTS SUCH AS YEARS OF EXERIENCE OR DEGREES CAN CRIPPLE A COMPANY'S TALENT ACQUISITION

Hiring the Best of the Bunch?

Perhaps the most common source of Bad Hires is the tendency to hire the *best of the bunch*. The mistake begins with the assumption that within the pool of job candidates there must be a winner. The interviewers compare the candidates and from that experience, they pick the "best" one. Even if that candidate is indeed the "best" one, the question is whether or not they are the quality of candidate needed in the job.

> **Example:** A client that had been named the best employer in the state and who had an excellent business with tremendous potential presented five candidates who had been selected from a pool of over 100. The position was for a senior-level executive in a role that was key to company's future. They wanted them tested in order to make the final decision. The results clearly showed that none of them were outstanding. The client asked us to interview them, questioning how the assessment results could be so low. Our interviews confirmed that none of the five were suitable for the role. The client maintained that these five were "without a doubt, the best ones they found." They had fallen into the trap of comparing candidates to each other and not to the needs of the position. The lack of success with previous hires had also led them to believe that talent was hard to find. They had lost sight of the desirability of jobs in their company. Changing the sourcing of the candidates brought

in a much higher level of talent, and with a new focus on what was needed, with the help of DATA, the position was successfully filled.

Losing Sight of "Good"

If companies use ineffective hiring methods for an extended period of time, they will accumulate a workforce of mediocre talent. What is worse, they may come to believe that is normal in their industry or in their area.

Example: A car manufacturer was trying to understand why they had low sales throughout one of their regions. They had little turnover and a strong sales training program. New salespeople were hired through an extensive interview process. The first step was to test the current sales team in 20 of their dealerships. When the results were analyzed, they discovered that few of their top salespeople would have been hired by the leading dealerships of other brands. Over the years, the bar for selection had been lowered bit by bit, until mediocre or non-performance had become the norm. Using DATA prevents this, as the next section of the book will explain.

IF COMPANIES USE
INEFFECTIVE HIRING METHODS
FOR AN EXTENDED PERIOD OF TIME,
THEY WILL ACCUMULATE
A WORKFORCE OF
MEDIOCRE TALENT.
WHAT IS WORSE,
THEY MAY COME TO BELIEVE
THAT IS NORMAL
IN THEIR INDUSTRY.

CHAPTER 4

IDENTIFYING THE JOB BEHAVIORS

It is important to unbundle the concepts into clear job behaviors and that they can be prioritized so as to better target your best hires.

Unbundle the Job

Jobs consist of sets of specific *job behaviors*. The first step in eliminating Bad Hires is to unbundle the job into its individual *job behaviors*. For example, the coffee shop does not want to hire a barista. They want a certain set of *job behaviors*:

- Greeting customers with a smile
- Listening to get the details of the customer's order
- Handling the transaction accurately
- Making the coffee drinks consistently according to the recipe
- Keeping the work area organized and clean
- Dealing with the stress when it is busy

There may be others. The key point is that the coffee shop wants to **rent** these job behaviors. When jobs are understood as the **renting of a specific set of job behaviors**, it becomes much easier to determine if a candidate can deliver those behaviors.

When an employee is hired, in effect, the company is renting their behaviors. For example, upscale hotels often offer a beakfast buffet, with an omelet station, where a chef will prepare whatever type of omelet you prefer. What behaviors are the hotel *renting* from that chef?

- A smiling greeting to every guest
- Consistent omelet making
- Reacting positively to unplanned requests
- Handling a routine job day after day

- Standing and not sitting down between omelets

Now, if the candidate for that job could not deliver all of these behaviors, would the hotel accept:

- An impersonal but consistent omelet maker?
- A smiling chef who sometimes makes good omelets and sometimes makes bad ones, but who enjoys the routine of the job?
- A consistently good omelet maker who hates to be interrupted by guests and shows it?

WHEN JOBS
ARE UNDERSTOOD
AS THE RENTING
OF A SPECIFIC SET
OF JOB BEHAVIORS,
IT BECOMES MUCH EASIER
TO DETERMINE
IF A CANDIDATE
CAN DELIVER
ON THOSE BEHAVIORS.

Is It Critical or Important or Just Nice to Have?

Not all job behaviors have the same level of importance. An effective illustration of this is found in looking at the job of a shortstop in baseball. That position involves several things:

- Catching pop flies
- Handling ground balls
- Throwing to first base
- Batting
- Running the bases
- Talking to the pitcher
- Wearing the uniform

Three of these are **Critical**:

- Catching pop flies
- Handling ground balls
- Throwing to first base

Failing to perform any one of these functions disqualifies a player from playing the position of shortstop.

Two other factors are **Important:**

- Batting
- Running the bases

Performing these functions makes the player a better shortstop. Lacking them does not prevent the person from playing shortstop, and there are many defensive shortstops that are excellent with the **Critical** factors, but are not particularly good at either of the **Important** factors. As for the **Other** factors, talking to the pitcher is nice, and looking good in the uniform is great for the baseball cards. These are the *nice to have*.

How Job Behaviors Changed the Hiring Model

Since the 90's, the three circle model has been a mainstay of effective hiring. Companies intent on hiring the right person collected an assortment of information that varied dramatically in accuracy and reliability. The model helped to sort out this information to obtain what was seen as a picture of the total person. The assessment part of this information was generally in the form of a comparison between the job candidate and a profile compiled by testing a selection of "top performers" in the particular job. (To learn more, see *Not Your Best Profile* at www.aboutassessments.com). While the assessment information was usually the most meaningful, it was difficult to sort out the key elements from those that were less important. Hiring decisions were often complicated, as different facts about the candidate were weighed against other facts. Too often it was assumed that good qualities would balance out the questionable ones.

Understanding the individual job behaviors in a particular position and knowing which ones are **Critical** is the first step in avoiding Bad Hires. This enables you to screen out job candidates that lack any of the **Critical** factors needed to perform that job successfully. Once that is done, you can now use the **Important** and **Other** factors plus additional information to select the best candidate for the position.

BestWork DATA's ability to describe individual job behaviors transformed the three circle model of job performance into a much more effective model for eliminating bad hires (see Illustration E).

Illustration E. Screen First, Then Select.

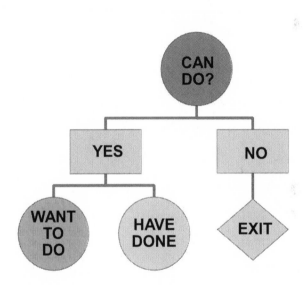

The question of whether or not a job candidate can perform the **Critical** job behaviors for a particular job was easily answered. If they **can** then the next step was to proceed with collecting and reviewing additional information in resumés, interviews, references and other sources. If the candidate **cannot** perform the **Critical** job behaviors, then they can be exited from the selection process at that time, without proceeding with interviews and more. None of that information can alter the fact that that particular candidate is a Bad Hire for that particular job. All of the candidates passing through this screening, meaning they have the strengths and abilities to deliver the **Critical** job behaviors, are OK's or average performers or Stars or excellent performers. The Bad Hires have been screened out.

It is easy to see how recognizing the **Critical** job behaviors can be a powerful advantage in screening and selecting the right people for the right jobs. It also focuses the hiring decisions on actual performance elements rather than less relevant facts, such as degrees and years of experience. These may be contributing information, but only after the **can do** questions have been answered.

Sounds "Good" But...

There are many ways to describe the ideal candidate for a particular job. Too often, the description focuses on intangibles, such as:

- strong values
- fits in with our culture
- winning attitude
- team player
- passion for the business
- determined
- dependable

These are all admirable qualities that would be welcome in any hire. Unfortunately, while they can be applauded, they cannot be measured reliably. Truly useful job descriptions must be stated in behavioral terms. In fact, a powerful axiom for both hiring and management is this: "If it cannot be described in behavioral terms, it is just a complaint." This could be modified for hiring: "If a critical hiring factor cannot be described in behavioral terms, it is just a wish."

The Tricky World of Desirable Concepts

Job postings are often laden with wonderfully-sounding descriptions, such as *dependable, customer-focused, self-starter* and *team player*. Certainly all of these characteristics are desirable, but the question is how to determine whether or not a candidate has those characteristics. The challenge is that each of those terms covers a broad range of interpretations. Some are actually misleading in the world of actually measuring human traits and abilities. When using a descriptive term like a concept, it is helpful to answer the question, "What behaviors are you describing with that term?" or "What behaviors do you want to see in that job?"

IF A CRITICAL HIRING FACTOR CANNOT BE DESCRIBED IN BEHAVIORAL TERMS, IT IS JUST A WISH.

These examples will illustrate the various interpretations of these terms:

Dependable

- Joe is *dependable*. He always follows the procedures.
- Ed is *dependable*. He always knows when to make an exception.
- Mary is *dependable*. I don't have to tell her what to do.
- Sam is *dependable*. He always follows instructions.
- Ellen is *dependable*. She is always on time.
- Bob is *dependable*. I can always call on him at the last minute.

All of these may be desirable but knowing which ones are most important is critical to identifying them in candidates.

Self-Starter

- John always figures out how to do it.

- Nicole doesn't wait for instructions.

- Ron has a great sense of urgency.

- Greg is self-motivated.

- Susan doesn't wait for everything to be just "right." She gets it done.

There are many versions of *self-starters.*

Team Player

- Robert takes charge and leads his team.

- Lou is there for whatever the team needs.

- Paula is a friend to everyone here.

- Mitch does it our way all the time.

- We never hear a complaint from Neil.

What role does the team need them to play?

Customer-Oriented

- Barbara is so friendly with our customers.

- David does anything to help a customer.

- Tammy believes the customer is always right.

- Ann understands how a customer feels.

- Phil never disagrees with a customer.

It is possible to find candidates who can deliver various job behaviors at an acceptable level but they may not excel at the ones most important to you. It is important to unbundle the concepts into clear job behaviors so that they can be prioritized so as to better target your best hires.

Case Study: How Creative Do You Want?

A large manufacturer and distributor of pens and other promotional products wanted to hire a director of marketing. Their business was based on a combination of outbound calls, mailings and email promotions. It was a fairly straightforward promotion plan that had been successful for many years, and the principal marketing factors were monitoring the volume of contacts, the effectiveness of each method and the efficiency of the system. The job posting however, emphasized "creativity". This attracted some highly-talented marketing professionals who saw an opportunity to exercise their own remarkable creativity. The company loved the concept of "creativity" and quickly hired their new director of marketing. Unfortunately, that was when everyone learned the many interpretations of "creativity". The new director's ideas were seen as disruptive to the core of the business, and he was advised to focus on the fundamentals of their standard promotions. Both parties realized that it was a bad match and soon parted ways.

BestWork DATA was then used to select the next director of marketing. The key difference is shown on the scale below which compares the range of creativity of the failed choice (A) to that of the choice that was ultimately successful in that role (B).

Chart 1. Comparing Creative Range of Two Candidates

Extreme Creativity; Totally Different Ideas	A				B		Limited Creativity; Improve Existing Ideas

Other examples of this include the Fortune 100 senior executive brought into a highly entrepreneurial company. Where once they had a large supporting staff, their role was now more hands on. Where once there was a slow bureaucratic decision making process, the emphasis was now on independent thinking and faster decisions. The same habits and experience that had enabled the Fortune 100 executive to thrive in the large scale corporate world were obstacles in the new position.

CHAPTER 5

DEFINING THE JOB WITH BEHAVIORS

Companies need the right behaviors in each job that can been seen and managed.

Compared to All of the Others...

In sports, teams want the strongest, the quickest and the toughest. Of course, every team cannot have All-Stars in every position, and if their game plan depended on having them, it would be a disappointing season. Businesses sometimes create strategies that depend on having a complete team of extraordinary and exceptional employees. Just as in sports, it is rarely possible to have a team of all All-Stars in business. Therefore, just as in sports, knowing an individual's specific strengths and abilities and the specific areas in which they need support is critical. DATA gives you that level of information.

BestWork DATA shows where an individual's strengths are compared to everyone else in the population. Is that strength common and easy to find in job candidates? Is it special and hard to find? The bell curve in Illustration F shows the normal distribution of any personality trait or cognitive ability within the working population.

Illustration F. Normal Distribution in the U.S.A.

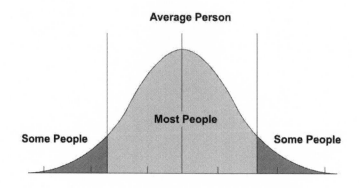

There are extremes at each end of the curve, but most people fall into the middle range of any trait or ability. Knowing the distribution of strengths in the population is important when planning the staffing for some roles. For example (with extremely conservative numbers):

- 75% of the population cannot persuade people to make buying decisions. They cannot close sales.
- 75% of the population cannot direct the actions of other people. They cannot manage them effectively.
- 25% of the population cannot consistently follow rules, policies or procedures.
- 50% of the population are unlikely to call out a problem if they see it.
- 50% of the population are not strategic thinkers. They have difficulty projecting the consequences of today's decisions into the future.
- 25% of the population struggle with change.
- 25% of the population cannot work accurately with details.
- 25% of the population cannot follow a detailed quality process.
- 25% of the population will not consistently follow safety procedures.
- 50% of the population is not innovative to any real degree.
- 25% of the population struggle in customer-facing roles, even though they seemed fine in the interview.

IT IS CRITICAL TO KNOW AN INDIVIDUAL'S SPECIFIC STRENGTHS, ABILITIES AND SPECIFIC AREAS IN WHICH THEY NEED SUPPORT.

Some key positions in businesses demand extreme strengths in several areas. Extreme strengths mean there are fewer people in the population who have them. With every added extreme, the population of viable candidates shrinks.

Case Study: Not Enough Talent to Go Around

A company sold a sophisticated technology solution that required an extended complex sales process. They had divided the country into seven territories that reflected the existing and potential customers for their solution. Over a period of three years, they had never had all of the seven positions filled. In fact, it was normal for only four to be filled at any time. The company paid well and was a positive place to work. A DATA analysis of the job provided an explanation of the problem.

As configured, the sale required the following:

- Top 25% speed of learning and information processing
- Top 25% control of the sales process and ability to handle objections
- Top 25% delivering high energy sales presentations
- Top 25% planning and coordinating the details and follow up
- Top 25% individually competitive and motivated by commission sales
- Top 25% adapting solution to prospect's needs

Each additional extreme added to the scarcity of candidates. Not only were they scarce, they were in demand by every company with a similarly complex solution sale. Recruiters were constantly hunting down such talent and hiring them away for more money or more benefits. It was a losing game with the positions and responsibilities designed as they were.

The solution was to reduce the number of territories to three, with a key salesperson over each of them. Supporting these three was a team of sales support specialists. The support team did not require the extreme strengths of the key salesperson, and their support freed up the salesperson to handle the extended territories. The support people were not highly recruited and were relatively easy to find. In this way, the company was able to retain the salespeople and have a stable sales strategy.

When designing a job without DATA, there is a tendency to ask for superlative characteristics. Most jobs do not need that. **DATA provides a way to craft many jobs into definitions that are more readily filled and often at a lower cost.**

What You Really Want Is Behavior

It is common to hear companies talk about the importance of building a *culture* or finding employees who fit in with their *culture*. While that sounds good and makes sense on the surface, what is actually wanted is a certain behavior. Companies need the right behaviors in each job, and lacking a way to define those in a practical way, they talk about it in terms of culture, or teamwork, dedication, leadership or some other desirable characteristic. BestWork DATA helps translate those concepts into the desired behaviors that can be seen and managed.

Job Behaviors Identified by Using BestWork DATA

The job behavior descriptions available from BestWork DATA enable an individual's specific strengths and abilities to be separated from the generalities of previous job titles and experience into factors that can be directly related to the needs of the present job. BestWork DATA has worked with clients to develop specific sets of reports for a wide range in industries. Within these sets are Job Reports for many of the specialized roles within industries. Each Job Report features the job behaviors that are common to that industry and to each job. A sampling of those job behaviors is provided for a variety of industries. The actual reports contain many more. You can see how any candidate can perform each of the various parts of the job. They may do some very well and struggle with others. You now have the information to see if that combination works for what you need.

Jobsmith™

BestWork DATA offers an easy to use online tool called Jobsmith™ that will help you describe the job behaviors for any job in just a few minutes. It will also enable you to identify the behaviors as being Critical, Important or Nice to Have for performing that job successfully. The lists below will help you to see various job behaviors that are found in different types of jobs.

Sales
- Ability to close sales
- Ability to handle complex or solution sales
- Ability to get appointments
- Ability to network effectively
- Ability to follow up effectively
- Ability to follow a sales script or sales path consistently
- Ability to respond to individual competition as a motivator
- Ability to negotiate
- Ability to build customer relationships
- Ability to learn complex product knowledge
- Ability to handle sales rejection
- Most effective sales cycle
- Ability to make effective presentations
- Ability to qualify prospects

Management
- Ability to direct the actions of others
- Ability to give effective feedback
- Ability to delegate responsibility
- Ability to plan effectively
- Ability to handle change
- Ability to follow rules and procedures consistently
- Ability to handle tactical issues
- Ability to think strategically
- Ability to handle routine
- Ability to handle details
- Ability to handle stress
- Sense of urgency
- Ability to listen
- Ability to motivate employees
- Ability to solve problems

Call Center
- Ability to handle inbound calls
- Ability to move customers to make buying decisions
- Ability to communicate enthusiasm
- Ability to empathize
- Ability to recommend products and services to customers
- Ability to handle rejection
- Ability to handle collections
- Ability to handle details of calls
- Ability to follow call scripts consistently
- Ability to handle routine
- Ability to solve problems
- Ability to work at a desk for long periods
- Ability to handle angry customers
- Ability to communicate warmth and friendliness

Restaurant
- Front of house or back of house
- Ability to be warm and friendly with guests
- Ability to deal with awkward situations or difficult guests
- Ability to follow service standards consistently
- Ability to notice service details

- Ability to follow recipes consistently
- Ability to handle stress
- Ability to control the guests' experience
- Ability to make recommendations for guests
- Ability handle routine tasks
- Ability to learn product knowledge
- Ability to organize work area
- Service attitude

Manufacturing
- Ability to recognize quality details
- Ability to follow quality standards
- Ability to follow safety rules and procedures consistently
- Ability to make quality decisions
- Ability to handle change
- Ability to handle routine
- Ability to solve problems
- Ability to work without distractions
- Ability to handle stressful work environments
- Ability to supervise others

Trucking
- Ability to follow traffic laws consistently
- Ability to handle the routine of long haul driving
- Ability to handle detailed paperwork
- Ability to follow procedures consistently
- Ability to interact with customers in a friendly manner
- Ability to handle the stress of short delivery driving
- Ability to manage time efficiently
- Ability to comply with safety rules and regulations consistently

Retail
- Willingness to engage customers
- Ability to follow merchandising standards consistently
- Ability to move customers to make buying decisions
- Ability to make recommendations
- Ability to follow procedures consistently
- Ability to organize work areas

- Ability to handle details
- Ability to manage others
- Ability to handle difficult customers

Banking
- Ability to be warm and friendly with customers
- Ability to handle details accurately
- Ability to follow security rules and standards consistently
- Ability to follow bank procedures consistently
- Ability to recommend service and products to customers

Healthcare
- Ability to communicate warmth and friendliness to patients
- Ability to follow patient care procedures consistently
- Ability to notice details of patient care
- Ability to call out problems
- Ability to handle stress of patient care
- Ability to make decisions
- Ability to handle the routine of patient care
- Ability to handle difficult patients
- Ability to handle detailed paperwork

IT Positions
- Ability to write error-free code
- Ability to follow existing conventions
- Ability to architect complex programs
- Ability to create innovative solutions
- Ability to call out problems
- Sense of urgency in completing projects
- Ability to operate with consistent standards for delivery of projects

Marketing/Advertising
- Range of creativity
- Ability to sell ideas
- Ability to plan effectively
- Ability to run a consistent campaign
- Ability to understand analytics
- Ability to think strategically

Automobile Dealers
- Ability to sell cars
- Ability to understand complex product knowledge
- Ability to move customers to make buying decisions
- Ability to engage walk in customers
- Ability to follow sales paths
- Ability to follow up with sales prospects
- Ability to sell financial and other services

Franchises
- Ability to follow franchise procedures and standards consistently
- Ability to direct the actions of others
- Ability to engage customers directly
- Ability to sell products or services
- Ability to organize operations

Construction
- Ability to supervise workers
- Ability to interact with clients
- Ability to enforce safety standards and procedures
- Ability to manage projects
- Ability to inspect details of projects
- Ability to estimate accurately
- Ability to solve problems
- Ability to handle complex projects
- Ability to handle routine projects

Financial Services
- Ability to accurately handle details
- Ability to accurately follow procedures
- Ability to call out problems
- Ability to sell services
- Ability to interact with clients
- Ability to challenge decisions
- Ability to think strategically

Staffing
- Ability to work short term assignments
- Ability to work with little direction
- Ability to handle routine
- Ability to learn new situations quickly
- Ability to interact with customers
- Ability to follow procedures consistently
- Ability to follow safety rules and guidelines consistently

Entrepreneurs/Startups
- Ability to interact with customers
- Ability to handle multiple roles
- Ability to sell products or services
- Ability to improvise
- Ability to handle change
- Ability to manage others
- Ability to organize operations

BestWork DATA offers easy-to-understand descriptions of hundreds of specific job behaviors developed over many years and through working with thousands of people in actual work situations. The JobSmith™ application will enable anyone to quickly create a new Job Report for any type of position. The possibilities are endless. If there are questions about job performance, BestWork DATA can usually help you answer it.

Using Scary Percentages vs. DATA to Define Your Hiring Targets
Hiring the right person for the right job at the most basic level is a game of percentages. DATA on the hard-wired personality traits and cognitive abilities gives you insight into how challenging a particular search might be.

These percentages refer to approximately how many people overall could fit your needs. Your number is also dependent on your location, competition from other companies' hiring efforts and other factors in your situation. Please note that these are the conservative percentages. There are always exceptions. Hoping that the iffy candidate you hire is one of those exceptions is a chancy business strategy.

- 50% of people cannot sell anything that requires persuasion.
- Only 25% can sell to senior level executives.
- 50% of people will do a good job if people do what they tell them to do.
- 50% of people will do a good job if someone will tell them what to do.
- 50% of people lose energy when interacting with others.
- 50% of people gain energy when interacting with others.
- 25% of people have a "right way" to do things.
- 25% of people adapt the situation to make that "right way" work.
- 25% of people adapt the way to the situation.

HOPING

THAT THE

IFFY CANDIDATE

YOU HIRE

IS ONE

OF THOSE EXCEPTIONS

IS A CHANCY

BUSINESS STRATEGY

CHAPTER 6

SCREEN FIRST... BEFORE YOU SELECT

A classic problem in hiring has been the focus on finding top performers.

The Pool of Candidates

Illustration G represents the pool of job candidates for any type of job. Within that population, there are some candidates that are ideally suited for that job (Stars), with all of the Critical job behaviors plus most of the Important ones. Stars often become top performers. There are also quite a few candidates that have the Critical job behaviors for the job plus some of the Important ones (OK's). Their performance is generally acceptable. There are also a set of candidates who lack one or more of the Critical job behaviors for this job (OOPS). They may have all of the Important ones, and they may be wonderful, hard-working people, but they cannot perform the job behaviors necessary for success in this particular job.

Illustration G. The Pool of Job Candidates

A classic problem in hiring has been the focus on finding top performers (Stars). It is difficult, if not impossible to identify what makes an individual a potential Star. The real difference between Stars and OK's lies in many intangible factors, such as work ethic, attitude, personal standard of excellence, dedication and more. These elements are not reliably measurable.

Countless assessment companies have presented profiling strategies as the means to identify Stars. By testing "top performers" in a certain job, they create a "template" or "success profile" for that job. Logically, that pattern could then be used to evaluate potential candidates for that job by comparing their scores to those of the "top performers". It almost works. It does identify some candidates who go on to perform at a satisfactory level. Unfortunately, it also brings in candidates who are almost right. They are only lacking one, and sometimes more, of the Critical job behaviors. Too often, they can almost be successful, and because that success seems to be in reach, time, energy and money are spent to close a gap that cannot be closed. (NOTE: for a more complete explanation and examples of how this happens, see the Appendix under *The Myth and Misses of Profiling*).

A Simple & Practical Solution

While DATA on the hard-wired traits and abilities of job candidates cannot accurately predict their success, it can definitely identify those candidates who lack the CRITICAL factors necessary for success in any type of job. For example:

- Salespeople who cannot move prospects to make a buying decision
- Financial workers who cannot work accurately with detailed information

- Customer-facing associates who cannot be friendly to customers
- Workers who cannot handle the extended routine of certain jobs
- Managers who understand the immediate but not the strategic
- Workers who cannot follow safety rules and regulations
- Employees who cannot handle change and the need for flexibility

FIRST,

REMOVE THE OOPS.

THEN YOU SELECT

BETWEEN THE

STARS AND OK's.

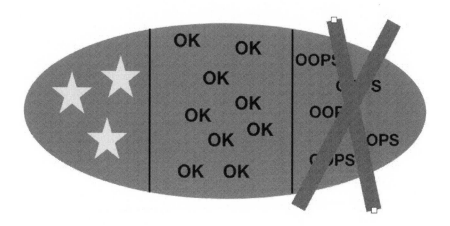

First Remove the OOPS

Looking again at the population of job candidates, including Stars, OK's and OOPS, it is easy to see a more practical and pragmatic application of DATA in Illustration H. If the OOPS are screened out first, the only candidates left are either OK's or Stars. The major source of Bad Hires has been eliminated. Of course, there is still much to be learned about the remaining candidates before making a selection. The DATA will also help in evaluating their potential, along with interviews, resumés, background checks and other information.

Case Study: Controlling the Quality of Decentralized Hiring

The owner of 40 fast food franchise stores had a major turnover and performance problem in the stores. The managers of each store made their own hires, and being busy and in need of help, they often made the quick and easy choices. Their choices were generally based on interviews without any quality DATA-level information.

The owner introduced BestWork DATA as a basic part of their application process for 100% of all job applicants. The DATA first screened out those applicants who could not consistently follow the operational procedures of the franchise. The DATA then sorted the remaining candidates into front of house (customer-facing) or back of house (not customer-facing). Each manager then had a pool of acceptable candidates from which they were welcome to select whomever they wished after the interviews. After several months of using the BestWork DATA system, the owner asked HR for the latest turnover numbers. Their reply was that it was negligible in terms of losing the hires made with the DATA.

Case Study: Handling a High Volume of Candidates

A major construction company typically received over 400 applications whenever they posted a job opening for a project manager. The problem of sorting through these was enormous, slowing down the selection process and doing nothing to increase the likelihood of acquiring top talent. BestWork DATA was included as part of their application process for all applicants. An automatic screen was set up to filter out those candidates who were not able to handle the extremely complex projects that were the principal business of the company. They also required extreme attention to details, so those applicants lacking that strength were filtered out. Lastly, the candidates who could not deal with confrontation and direct the actions of others easily were eliminated. The candidates that were screened out may have been wonderful people, well-educated and hard-working, but they lacked the CRITICAL strengths and abilities that were necessary for the job in question. They may have been perfect for any number of other jobs, but not that particular one. Once the system was in place, it typically screened out over 300 of the 400+ applicants. It kept all of those people from becoming a Bad Hire and from spending their time in the wrong job for them.

Case Study: Hiring an Executive Assistant

The CEO of a manufacturing company wanted to hire an executive assistant. The ad was posted and in a matter of a few days, over 200 candidates applied. The CEO was overwhelmed; she had planned to interview the candidates but she never expected that level of response. After first considering to outsource the interviews, she contacted BestWork DATA. Executive assistants must match their executive in two critical areas:

- **Speed of learning and processing information** – the candidates can be faster but they cannot be slower. Misunderstandings and incomplete communication would result, requiring the executive to repeat instructions and take additional time to explain instructions.
- **Level of assertiveness** – the candidates must be higher or the same as the executive. If the assistant is less assertive, they will not want to ask too many questions, even if they do not fully understand something. They will also not challenge the executive, even when the executive makes a mistake.

IMPORTANT NOTE: BestWork DATA already has these factors identified for hundreds of jobs. Clients do not have to know them or figure them out. The reports contain that information.

Using those two areas as screening factors with the DATA, the 200 candidates were quickly reduced to twenty and experience factors pared that number to seven. The CEO found the assistant she wanted in that group.

CHAPTER 7

NOW, SELECT THE BEST CANDIDATE

The candidate's DATA can be used toward any type of job and our instruments represent the current state of the art in both the psychology and the psychometrics.

The Parts of the Selection Decision

Once the Bad Hires have been screened out, all of the other candidates CAN do the job. Now the focus becomes selecting the candidates that are best suited for the job. DATA is an important tool for that, along with other things such as interviews, references, resumés, skills testing,

BestWork DATA – A Simple Solution

While there are over 80,000 occupationally-related assessments in the marketplace, the vast majority are outdated, both in terms of the psychological science used for their models and the psychometric science used in their instruments. Only a handful combine both cognitive and personality measurement, both of which are essential to any understanding of job performance. BestWork DATA's instruments represent the current state of the art in both the psychology and the psychometrics. The practical usability of the information in the BestWork DATA system is a disruptive innovation in the world of human capital management. The ease of use, the pricing and the scope of application gives businesses extraordinary tools to fully realize the potential of their employees.

BestWork DATA does not require or depend upon testing top performers as did the old profiling methodology, and BestWork needs no special training or expert interpretation. In less than 30 minutes, the DATA is available in a menu of applications that anyone can use and understand. Lastly, the cost is a fraction of other products, reflecting the digital nature of the system. BestWork's unlimited license enables the company to use it with 100% of its applicants with a minimal cost per candidate. This simplifies the process by making the DATA available first for screening and then for selecting the ones for interviews. Once a final set of candidates has been chosen, the DATA can then be used for specific comparisons among the finalists.

Virtual Interview Text

BestWork DATA's online experience gathers a set of DATA that describes how an individual will perform the various job behaviors of any type of job. BestWork DATA then translates the DATA into easy descriptions of how that individual will perform a specific job behavior, such as *closing a sale* or *working with detailed information*. The descriptions are easily understood without special training or help from experts. There are over two thousand different job behavior descriptions. The text uses the terminologies of the industries in which the particular jobs are found. The comprehensive format of the Job Reports not only makes hiring decisions more effective, but the full descriptions enable hiring managers to recognize many more performance characteristics such as:

- Fit with different managers.
- Time to reach a level of productivity.
- Training and support needs.
- Fit with different work groups.

Case Study: Choosing Between Two Qualified Candidates

A bank created a new executive position for an important expanding part of their business. The Bad Hires lacking the critical strengths for the role had been screened out, and interviews had narrowed the final choices down to two candidates. Both candidates had the necessary experience for the job. It came down to the DATA to pick the best one. Chart 2 below shows the key difference between the two candidates.

Chart 2. Comparing Need for Structure in Two Candidates

Flexible & Adaptable; Can Work Without Clear Procedures		A			B		Must Know "Right Way"; Needs Clear Procedures & Structure

Candidate A was flexible, needing few procedures and able to adjust to the needs of each situation. Candidate B had to know the "right way" to do things, needing clear procedures and a structure to guide them. As this was a new position without any existing structure or procedures, the DATA made the decision easy. Candidate A could start right away. The interesting point is that Candidate B was probably the best candidate once the position was established, but was definitely not right at the time of the decision.

IMPORTANT NOTE: The factors shown in the Case Studies are examples pulled from existing BestWork DATA reports. Clients do not have to figure them out.

Case Study: Selecting for the Reporting Relationship

A company was seeking a COO to support the CEO, who was wonderfully innovative but who needed a more structured focus for their ideas. Four candidates were selected as having the right experience and having done well in the interviews. The scale below shows the information processing speed for the CEO and each of the candidates.

Chart 3. Comparing Processing Speed Among Candidates

Processes Information Slowly		A	B		CEO C	D	Processes Information Quickly

Candidates A and B are not a good match for the CEO, as they process information much more slowly, despite having the same level of experience and a similar set of skills.

This left candidates C and D who were both a good match with the CEO in terms of processing speed. Their critical difference is shown in the scale following.

Chart 4. Comparing Attitude Toward Change Among Candidates

Making Changes	CEO		D			C	Limit Changes

Candidate C is at the opposite end of the scale from the CEO, wanting to limit and even avoid changes. A difference this great is only going to generate debates and arguments. Candidate D is more moderate in viewing changes, and this can be a reasonable counterpoint to the CEO. (The interesting anecdote to this example is that the board of directors had interviewed each of these candidates and reviewed their resumés. Their recommended hire was Candidate B, followed by Candidate A. Their third place choice was Candidate C. Candidate D was hired and did a magnificent job.) The depth of information that is available with BestWork DATA reveals choices that are not visible without it.

Really...How Easy Is It to Understand?

In the early days of BestWork DATA, a new client called a few days after purchasing the system. He explained that he was making a crucial hire for a persuasive sales position, and he could not afford to make a mistake; therefore, he wanted someone to walk him through his first candidate's report. The client support person assured him that she was happy to do so, and she asked him to read the first line of the report for her. He read, "Has difficulty persuading prospects to take action; cannot close persuasive sales." There was a pause after he finished, and he said, "I think I've got this. Sorry for the call."

It Is This Easy...

These descriptions from BestWork DATA Job Reports clearly point out the candidate's lack of ability to deliver typically critical job behaviors in each of the positions:

- **From the Financial Job Report** – Has difficulty following procedures consistently; sees reasons to make exceptions
- **From the Management Job Report** – Feedback given can be less direct and less specific when it is negative, limiting the ability of the person to adjust their behavior effectively
- **From the IT Position Job Report** – Takes shortcuts and makes exception to coding conventions; documentation can be incomplete and inconsistent
- **From the Customer Service Report** – Can be seen as cool and impersonal by others
- **From the Administrative Job Report** – Not organized in handling paperwork; works best with minimal paperwork

In contrast, the following are examples that would generally be considered to be positive confirmation of critical strengths in various jobs:

- **From a Project Manager Job Report** – Follow-up is usually timely and complete

- **From a Persuasive Sales Job Report** – Abilities are a match for selling solutions that depend upon more complex sales involvement

- **From a Senior Level Executive Job Report** – Energy and attention is generally focused on strategic and longer term opportunities

- **From a Fast Casual Restaurant Job Report** – Warm, friendly & welcoming with guests

- **From a Human Resources Job Report** – You are highly sensitive to the emotional signals of employees, which tells you about their morale

Evergreen Reports

Job candidates are rarely perfect. There are good things and not so good things. What works for one manager, may not work for the other. BestWork DATA shows you all of these, separately and distinctly. Another benefit of this is that the reports are essentially *evergreen*. They are not tied to the *profile* of a particular job. The candidate's DATA can be used to view any type of job. Candidates who may not fit the job for which they applied may be well-suited for one they did not know about. *The business now has a better way to mine for talent.*

The concepts within this book can be applied using other tools, but such applications can be problematical and the effectiveness questionable. The opportunity to experience BestWork DATA is included with this book. (See BestWork DATA Pilot Program at the end of the book.)

CHAPTER 8

THE TRUTH ABOUT INTERVIEWS

The power of DATA is that it enables poor interviewers to avoid bad hires and all interviewers to make better hires.

Interviews Don't Really Work the Way You Think They Do

Interviews have always been a cornerstone of the selection process, and they are still important. However, it is important to understand what can be learned in an interview and how accurate and reliable it is likely to be. While many managers or business owners feel that they have a *gift* for finding good hires, research shows that what they usually have is a *gift* for remembering the good hires and forgetting the bad hires. This is an example of a psychological phenomenon called *fading affect bias*, in which negative outcomes are forgotten more quickly than positive outcomes.

Some Scary Interviewing Facts

Unstructured interviews have conclusively been shown to be the worst way to evaluate or to predict how a job candidate will ultimately perform in the job. "A round up of 85 years of research by leadership scholars showed that unstructured interviews were ranked so low in effectiveness that they only explained 14% of an employee's performance." [10] Research has shown that interviewers make a subconscious decision on whether they are positive or negative about the candidate in less than two minutes. If they are positive, the rest of the interview is spent accumulating enough evidence to justify a positive decision. If they are negative, the rest of the interview is spent accumulating enough evidence to justify a negative decision. This is an example of a psychological phenomenon known as *confirmation*

[10] Hedges, Kristi. (2015 May. *Why Job Interviews Are Like Flipping A Coin* Forbes)

bias, in which one searches for, interprets and favors information that confirms one's pre-existing beliefs.

UNSTRUCTERED INTERVIEWS ARE THE WORST WAY TO EVALUATE OR TO PREDICT HOW A JOB CANDIDATE WILL PERFORM IN THE JOB.

An incredible majority of people feel that they can judge the candidate's capabilities and character in a personal meeting. Actually, what they do unconsciously is see how much the candidate is like themselves. This is an example of a psychological phenomenon called *similarity bias*, in which a person tends to prefer working with people who are most like themselves.

"It was a great interview. I really liked them from the start," said the recruiter. That is an example of *affinity bias*, in which the more the candidate is liked by the interviewer, the more likely they are to make a positive hiring decision. These biases are unconscious. It is helpful to understand them and to be aware of them, but it is impossible to completely avoid their influence on interviews.

What About the Professional Interviewers? They're Good, Right?
A group of 120 professional interviewers were surveyed regarding their success rates on making good hires. The group used the latest tactics and methodologies for their interviews, sharing the best practices with their peers. They dealt with executive positions, typically in sales or management. The question they were asked was, "Thinking back on the many times in which you have made hiring decisions based on your interviewing of those candidates, and particularly of those times in which your success rate was exceptional, what was it?" In other words, when they were really good, what was the "really good" rate? Their answer was that three out of four were good hires. It is important to note that this was the "exceptional" rate. They were then asked what was their average rate. That answer was about 60% or six right out of 10 hires. A small business will go out of business at that rate. It will struggle even with only one Bad Hire out of four. Considering that these were highly experienced and knowledgeable professional interviewers, who were constantly interviewing candidates, it is doubtful that most managers or business owners are going to match their performance. In many cases, the

quality of the pool of candidates which a business attracts has more to do with the quality of hires than the skills or insight of the interviewers.

The Interviewer and the Interviewee

Some interviewers are skilled and experienced; some are less so. Some interviewees are skilled and experienced at interviewing; some are less so. In addition to those variables, people tend to relate best to people who are most like themselves. In an interviewing situation, this means that the more the interviewee is like the interviewer, the better the interview will generally go. Unfortunately, the interviewer may have a set of strengths and abilities quite different than the ones required for the job in question.

Case Study: Call Center with Inbound Calls

A call center of 300 seats was experiencing a turnover rate of over 300%, despite careful interviewing of all candidates. In fact, the head of recruiting personally interviewed each of the final candidates. She was smart, experienced and dedicated to doing the job well. She was extremely well-organized, attentive to details and a stickler for punctuality. Naturally, she looks for similar characteristics in employees. She expected them to be on time; to be smartly groomed and neatly dressed; and to have any resumés or other materials to be detailed and organized. Candidates who met those standards were likely to be hired, and those who did not, were not hired. Ironically, that was the problem.

One of the critical job behaviors for the call center was the ability to answer hundreds of inbound calls from potential customers responding to advertisements. That is a fairly specialized ability, because about one third of the population cannot do that for an extended period time. They have a hard-wired personality trait that enables them to handle details, organize things and plan thoroughly. That ability to plan is also a need to plan and know what is happening next. They work best in a closely scheduled environment with few interruptions. The problem is that every inbound call is an interruption, an unplanned event. Each one of those calls causes stress, and it does not take many days with hundreds of these interruptions by the calls for the stress to reach a level that is just too much. The recruiter was doing her very best to hire the right people, and those were the ones wired with traits just like her. Unfortunately, that was exactly wrong for the job handling inbound calls. Once BestWork DATA was used to match candidates directly to the necessary job behaviors, turnover ceased to be a major issue.

The Perfect Interviewee & the Bad Hire

The information from DATA can describe the key job behaviors for any job, but what if that DATA was used to describe the *Perfect Interviewee,* not the perfect one for a particular job but the perfect one for delivering a great interview for almost any job. This is not imaginary. These people exist. Often the first clue is the resumé with eight sales jobs in seven years or the manager hired by six companies in six years. The job changes strongly suggest a performance issue, although the person clearly did not have a problem being hired again for a similar job. Here is what the DATA usually shows:

- Fast learning & processing speed – meaning quick recognition of what the interviewer is looking for and the ability to assemble the appropriate story on the spot

- Emotional sensitivity – enables the interviewee to read the emotions and reactions of the interviewer and adjust their attitude and delivery, even feeding back the same emotions

- High flexibility – an almost chameleon-like ability to present whatever characteristics are most desirable to the interviewer

- Ability to communicate energy and enthusiasm – all of the other elements broadcast in high definition color and surround sound

- Highly competitive – self-starter vibe; winning the next job is a competition for the interviewee

Regardless of this interviewee's ability to actually do the job, they will definitely be a strong candidate based on the interview. Without tools like BestWork DATA, such Bad Hires are unavoidable.

> **IMPORTANT NOTE:** The traits and abilities noted in the example above **ARE NOT** indicative of a Bad Hire for all jobs. In fact, those may be ideal for some jobs. The example is to demonstrate that there are job candidates who are essentially *hard-wired* to interview well. That is why DATA is necessary to look beyond the interview impressions.

Interview This Way & Interview That Way

There are hundreds of books on interviewing, countless YouTube videos and interview coaches are readily available. Still, most interviews are conducted by executives whose main job is something else entirely. Often they have had little training, and despite their best efforts, leave the interviews with little clear information with which to make important hiring decisions. Here are some suggestions:

1. **Behavioral event-based interview questions** – This type of question asks the candidate to refer to their past experience in answering the question rather than offering their opinions, feelings or thoughts. Example: Instead of "What do you think about change?" the question is "Give me an example from your previous experience in which you had to deal with a major change in your job." Research studies have shown that behavioral

event-based questions produce more reliable answers. An important caution is that interviewing books, classes and coaches often prepare their candidate students with strong answers to such questions. Still, that is the most effective type of question. One of the advantages of BestWork DATA is that behavioral event-based interviews are provided for each candidate, and those questions are based on each candidate's DATA. In a sense, these questions automatically target each candidate's weaknesses or areas that need clarification.

Example: Candidate A is interviewing for a persuasive sales position. The DATA shows that Candidate A is only comfortable dealing with moderate levels of confrontation. A question for Candidate A is: *How can you tell when you have tried to close a sale enough times?*
This question focuses directly on Candidate A's challenge in closing sales, which is not closing enough times. (Top salespeople in that type of sales position typically close nine or more times during their sales presentation.)

Candidate B is also interviewing for a persuasive sales position. The DATA shows that Candidate B is highly persuasive and is comfortable with an extremely high level of confrontation. A question for Candidate B is: *Give me an example from your experience, when you have pushed too hard for a sale.*

Unlike Candidate A, Candidate B has no trouble closing many times for the sale. B's challenge is to avoid pushing too hard for the sale, and that is the focus of their question.

Using BestWork DATA's interview questions also standardizes the interview process, although companies may choose to add questions of their own that may be specific to the job. This feature enables poor interviewer to deliver effective interviews and average interviewers to become quite good.

2. **Group interviews** – Interviewing multiple candidates at the same time is rarely effective. Lacking DATA about job behaviors, it becomes a kind of beauty contest and audition. Unfortunately, the characteristics that help one to excel in those situations is generally not the same as the ones needed for the job.

3. **Multiple interviewers** – It is sometimes important for the key people who will be working with the new employee to meet the candidates. Various executives are called on to interview candidates and the decisions discussed collectively. There is no doubt that different perspectives can be of value in some situations. It is important to understand the mechanics of the process, however. Each interviewer has their own set of positives and negatives. The collective effect of applying these different parameters to the candidates is to eliminate the extremes of each

trait or ability. One is too focused on details. Another seems too direct for one of the interviewers. Another is too competitive or too conservative or too loose. Before long, only the average candidates remain, having no traits too noticeable for any of the interviewers. The power of DATA is that it answers many of the questions that have previously been probed in the interviews. Once a candidate's job behaviors are known, there is no need to explore those areas. Interviews move to firmer ground, such as attitude, compatibility, sense of values, communication and other areas. An important component is "feeling right or not right". There is no way to scientifically explain it, but when a candidate does not "feel right", whatever the cause, they are not "right" for the company.

4. **Video interviews** – Video interviews have all the issues that live interviews have but with more expense. A percentage of people are uncomfortable in front of a camera. This has a significant effect on how they perform in a video interview. Conversely, some people love to be in front of a camera or an audience. This ability skews their video interview in a positive way. The use of DATA to screen out Bad Hires can eliminate much of that expense. Once the viability of the candidate is known, it becomes a simpler decision as to use a video interview first or bring the candidate in for the real thing.

5. **Clever questions interviews** – Some recruiters feel that asking clever questions gives them insight into a candidate's creativity and problem-solving ability. It can do that in some cases. If the candidate answered the question well, they are either a creative problem solver or a practiced interviewer who prepared for such questions. If the candidate did not answer well, they are possibly not a creative problem solver, or they are but they do not improv well or they want to consider the question from more different angles than the time allows or some other variant.

The True Value of Interviews

Interviews are fraught with problems, but once you know that the candidate has the hard-wired strengths and abilities to perform the job, you definitely want to interview them. Behavioral event-based interview questions, such as the ones provided by BestWork DATA, will help you to understand how the person will fit into the position and how to train and manage them. You will also meet them personally, where you will get a sense of who they are. It will be imperfect. The more they are different than you will affect your impressions greatly. It is important for you to consider the role that you want them to play, not how much they are like you. The DATA will help you to know that. It also gives them a chance to know you. It is important to recognize that both parties are trying to make the best decision.

A recent article in the New York Times observed that as the news media has become more digital, people access the news through a variety of ways. Unlike traditional newspapers where stories were researched and verified before publishing, digital information is frequently available instantly at the time of the event. One consequence of the immediacy of digital media is that people often read the opinions and commentaries before reading the actual news describing the events. Opinions are formed based on the commentaries and not the facts. When making hiring decisions, DATA and facts should always precede interviews. Too many times, engaging interviews with job candidates have led to doubts and questions about the facts shown by the DATA and other sources. Staring with those facts and DATA as a reference point will lead the interviews in the most effective directions.

CHAPTER 9

PUTTING THE PIECES TOGETHER

Using the DATA to screen out candidates that will ultimately not succeed at the job is foremost.

How to Put the Pieces Together

Successful hiring decisions depend upon several different kinds of information. Some of that information is objective and reliable. Some of it is subjective and much less reliable. Interview impressions can be personally powerful but not necessarily reliable. How to put the various pieces together into a logical and effective decision is an important key to avoiding Bad Hires. Relying on the DATA to screen out candidates that will ultimately not succeed at the job is foremost. After that is done, a simple summary sheet can be a practical means of organizing thoughts, opinions and impressions about each candidate in a format that makes comparisons among the candidates much easier. It has the advantage of collecting the interviewer's rating quickly and as close to the event as possible. It is not asking for an analysis, but immediate impressions, which are generally most accurate. In fact, research has shown that most interview decisions are made subconsciously within the first two minutes of the interview. If that decision was positive, the rest of the interview was spent trying to collect enough information to justify hiring the candidate. If the initial decision was negative, the rest of the interview was spent trying to collect enough information to justify not hiring the candidate. While this may not be true in all cases, the reality is that those first impressions are important and capturing the information while it is fresh is a good idea.

The Interview

In the interview, you are looking for four quick impressions:

- **First Impression** – In the first few minutes of meeting the candidate, what was your first impression? Was it, "Wow! This is going to be a great interview." Was it, "Oh, how long is this going to take?" Was it something in-between?

- **Grooming & Dress** – Is the candidate dressed appropriately for the job in question? Is their personal grooming right for that job? A coat and tie might be rated Much More Than Needed for a factory job, but maybe just Acceptable for an executive job. Jeans and a t-shirt might be rated Much Less Than Needed for that executive job but Acceptable for the factory.

- **Attitude During Interview** – What is their overall attitude during the interview? Positive and energetic? Quiet and not that responsive? Defensive?

- **Communication** – Does the candidate communicate at the level needed for the job in question? Are their grammar and language skills appropriate for the role?

These four checkpoints can usually be quickly and accurately evaluated by the interviewer, and each one is a key consideration in the hiring decision. This interview was the first time for both the company and the candidate to personally meet. A strong candidate will be prepared and put their best foot forward. How well they meet your expectations at this point is telling, both positively and negatively.

Skills, Education & Experience

The information for this section comes initially from the interview and resumé, but it may be explored and checked further if the candidate is moved forward in the selection process. At this point, the interviewer must use the information they have at hand without regard to what may come later.

- **Education** – Too often, job descriptions ask for degrees that are really unnecessary for the job. This is usually a misplaced effort aimed at getting more qualified candidates. With the exception of certain jobs that depend upon specialized knowledge acquired in university programs, the majority of jobs depend more on hard-wired traits and abilities along with the values and personal standards of the candidate.

- **General Experience** – General experience refers to the working experience of the candidate. This may include a variety of jobs, internships or part-time work. All of these contribute to the candidate's understanding of job responsibilities and working in a business. It is not always necessary to have exactly the same type of experience as with the job in question.

- **Specific Job Experience** – This is the place to capture how much experience the candidate has that is the same as with the job in question. With many hires out of college, there will be none. With the changes in technology occurring so rapidly, the same is not uncommon for many new jobs.

- **Special Training (Optional)** – This place allows the interviewer to capture any additional training that may be relevant to the job in question. If there is none, this section may be left blank.

Rules for Avoiding Bad Hires

1. Identify the specific job behaviors that need to be rented.

2. Rate these as Critical, Important or Other.

3. Screen out any candidates that lack one or more of the Critical factors.

4. Screen out any candidates who lack any specialized skills or knowledge that is also Critical for performing the job.

5. Use the Job Reports, resumés and interviews to select the best candidates from those that are remaining.

CHAPTER 10

NOW THAT THEY ARE HIRED...

A positive onboarding process is an important opportunity to build a strong relationship with new employees. DATA can help uncover the various things different employees need in order to be comfortable and become productive in their new job.

What's Next? Or Don't Drop the Ball Now

Now that the best candidate for the job has been found and hired, it is important to complete the hiring process and onboard the new employee. Many companies feel that was done when all the papers were signed and the employee manual was given to the new employee. Unfortunately, too often the new employee is shown to where they will work and left to figure out the rest on their own. After all of the recruiting efforts and the selection process that went into finding this person, would it make sense to make them feel welcome and comfortable in their new company? Or, you could follow the lead of a West Coast company that recruited a designer from the Southeast. The designer arrived at the company headquarters in Los Angeles, where an administrative assistant showed them to a vacant office with a desk and chair, explaining that this was their new office. The vice president who had hired them was not in and would not be in that week at all. The head of the design department was also away for a few days. There was no one who could suggest what the new designer should do in the meantime. Imagine the effect that this had on his enthusiasm and confidence in deciding to take the job.

Worse still was the manufacturing company who hired a new worker. They walked them through the plant, warning them about the dangers of the machines and cautioning them to stay clear of the robot carriers that moved through the aisles delivering parts. After being thoroughly educated on the dangers of wandering in the plant, the new employee worked diligently for the next five or six hours without a break. When the supervisor noticed this, he asked why he did not take a break. The new employee, somewhat embarrassed, replied that he did not know where either the restrooms or the break room were located, and he was afraid to go looking for them. Needless to say, an onboarding process was created and put into place to avoid such omissions.

Onboarding

Onboarding involves several simple elements that make a world of difference to new employees.

- Personally welcome the new employee. This can be done ideally by their manager or supervisor, but another person can also do it. This reinforces their decision to take the job, and sets a positive tone on the start of their new role.

- Show them around the work area or facility, so they know where things are, such as the restrooms, the break areas, where to get supplies, etc.

- While the formal hiring process usually includes work schedules, it is helpful to describe how the scheduling breaks and lunchtimes actually work. Include how the organization observes holidays or events, such as employee birthdays.

- Similarly, describe the normal way employees dress or any special grooming guidelines that may or may not be written down. For example, a company may have casual wear on Fridays.

- Make sure they have the things they need to do their job, such as pens, paper, stapler, etc. This includes any necessary passwords or access codes.
- Introduce the new employee to their coworkers and other employees or executives with whom they work.
- Explain any specialized terminology that is used in the company that may not be familiar to the new employee.
- Follow up with them after their first week to answer any questions or fill in things that may have been missed.

Have you ever been to a social event at which you really knew few if any of the other attendees, but you were greeted by a host who welcomed you, showed you where to go, where the food and drink was located and even introduced you to some of the other guests? Contrast that with the ones at which you were left to find your own way. Of course, both could turn out to be enjoyable, but there is a great deal of difference in the experience.

BestWork DATA includes a report, Onboarding Keys, that recommends specific onboarding keys for each individual employee based on their needs. Different employees need different things in order to be comfortable and become productive in their new job:

- Some need to fully understand all of the details of the job, while others are okay figuring them out along the way.
- Some have to know the "right way" to do things in their new job, even if the job has a great deal of flexibility. In their world,

there must be a "right way." Others can improvise on Day One.

- Some need extra time to learn new product knowledge or new procedures. Others "get it" right away.
- Some want to meet their coworkers so they can feel "at home." Others need to be settled first and comfortable in the job before meeting anyone.
- Some will gladly ask questions when they want to know something. Others hold back their questions, not wanting to show what they do not know.

The BestWork DATA Onboarding Keys Report shows you what is needed for each new employee.

New employees can find their own way most of the time. Smart companies have recognized that a positive onboarding process is an important opportunity to build a strong relationship with new employees. It makes them feel like part of the team, and that feeling encourages them to become productive much faster.

CHAPTER 11

AFTER THE HIRE...TRAINING

Training an existing or a new employee is one of the most powerful motivational tools. DATA is essential for any training to optimize its effectiveness.

And Now the Training...

New employees must often be trained in the skills or product knowledge needed to perform their new job. This is also true in the case of internal hires being promoted to new positions. There are two key things that must be considered. The obvious first thing is to provide the training that is necessary. Amazingly, this is not always the case. A not uncommon story is that of the company who used BestWork DATA to determine why one of their new supervisors was not performing satisfactorily in their new role. The DATA showed their strengths and abilities to be an excellent match with what was needed in the supervisory job. Clearly job fit was not the problem. The question was asked, "What training have they been given in supervisory skills?" The awkward answer was, "None." If it was golf, and they had received no instruction in playing golf, would it be surprising that they did not play golf well? They had selected a strong candidate for the supervisor position, but after the hire, they failed to provide the skill needed for the job.

It is important to recognize any special skills or product knowledge that is required for the performance of the job. *On the job training* is rarely effective for many reasons:

- Too often it is given by someone not skilled at training.
- The pace of business limits the opportunities for training.
- Training is occurring with *live clients* or *live prospects*, which is expensive in terms of opportunities and usually limits training in any case.

- It is not delivered in any traditional or proven training methodology.

Training an existing or a new employee is one of the most powerful motivational tools. It is a clear demonstration of the value of that individual.

Optimizing Training Results

DATA is essential for any training to optimize its effectiveness. The reality of the effectiveness of any training program is that one third of the participants typically do exceptionally well; one third do moderately well; and one third benefit very little, if at all, from the training. The reason for this is that the hard-wired traits and abilities of each individual determine what kind of training is most effective for them. Those critical factors are:

- **Speed of Learning** – Some people acquire new information and new skills quickly; others acquire that same information and those same skills at an average rate of speed; and another group learns much more slowly. No matter how the training class is taught, it is impossible to deliver the training in such a way as to include all learning speeds. Some will become bored and disinterested or some will be somewhat lost, depending upon how the class is delivered.

- **Need for Details** – Some people have a high need for the complete details of any subject in order for them to fully understand it, and therefore, be able to use the information and the training. Some people have very little need for details, and in fact, struggle with training programs that emphasize or require a lot of details. Each group optimizes their learning when the details of the training match with their needs. When the details are limited, the high need group is not comfortable applying the training. When the details are complete, the low need group loses interest and does not really engage with the training.

- **The *Right Way*** – There is a large group of the population who need to know exactly what the *right way* to do anything. In their world, there is one *right way* and that way must be fully understood before any action can be taken. An equally large group of the population tends to adjust their actions to the needs of the situation. They value flexibility and the idea of a *right way* is not possible for them. When training methodologies do not understand this and allow for it in their programs, the training is discounted to the extent that the approach is different than the hard-wired traits of the participants.

- **Any Questions?** – Half of the population is reluctant to ask any questions when they do not understand something in a training session. If the trainer is not aware of this and who those participants are, they may fail to recognize unanswered questions and misunderstandings within their training group.

THE REALITY OF

ANY TRAINING PROGRAM'S

EFFECTIVENESS IS THAT

ONE THIRD OF THE PARTICIPANTS

TYPICALLY DO EXCEPTIONALLY WELL;

ONE THIRD DO MODERATELY WELL;

AND ONE THIRD BENEFIT

VERY LITTLE, IF AT ALL,

FROM THE TRAINING.

Case Study: Training Needs Make the Choice

Hiring the right person is sometimes directly connected to how that person can be trained. A fairly large bank was hiring an executive for a new position that had been recently created. The selection process came down to two equally-qualified candidates, with the principal difference in each one's training needs. One candidate had a high need for details and for understanding exactly the *right way* to do the job. The second candidate needed few details and was comfortable with few guidelines. Given ample time to train the new executive for this new position, it was clear that the first candidate was best for the job. The bank, however, had no one to provide that training in the near future, yet they needed someone in the position right away. The first candidate needed training that was not available. The second candidate was acceptable, but not exceptional; however, they could start immediately without the training. Therefore, DATA enabled a more effective business decision by identifying how the training would impact the decision.

Making Training More Effective

Clearly, it is much easier to apply the training information in one-on-one situations. Still, when the costs of training programs are considered, along with the very real objectives of the training, the opportunity for applying DATA to larger initiatives is too promising to dismiss. Some possible options are:

- The group can be separated into sections based on speed of learning and the pace of training adjusted for each section.

- Handouts or additional materials can be made available for the participants who need more detailed information.

- Facilitators can use the DATA to identify the participants who will not join class discussions or ask questions. They can then proactively engage with them during the training.

- In many cases, the DATA can be used to identify the training areas that will be most beneficial to each individual.

- Conversely, the DATA can also be used to identify those issues with specific individuals that are unlikely to be improved with training.

CHAPTER 12

MANAGING THE NEW HIRE

Every hard-wired personality trait and cognitive ability affects the relationship and communication between the manager and each employee.

Manager & Employee…A Match?

The primary cause of poor job performance, or a Bad Hire, is the individual lacking the critical strengths needed to perform that job. When an individual's job performance is not satisfactory, and when they do have the strengths needed to perform the job, the next place to look is to see if they have the necessary training and materials to do the job. An equally-important factor is the match between the employee and their manager. Turnover studies surveying employees leaving companies found that in many cases the employees were leaving their manager, not the company. For them, the manager-employee relationship was not satisfactory. DATA offers a clear picture of the operational elements of that relationship. The requirements for the role of manager may be different than those for the employee. It is those differences which must be acknowledged and understood in order to avoid communication problems for both the manager and the employee. Each hard-wired trait and ability affects that relationship.

Speed of Processing Information & Speed of Communication

When one of the parties is either slower or faster than the other one, the onus is on the faster one to slow down their communication. The faster person tends to communicate at the same speed at which they learn and process information. They leave out some of the pieces when communicating, unconsciously believing that the other person will fill in the gaps as they would. Instead, that person misses part of the story or part of the instructions.

IMPORTANT NOTE: Speed of processing & communicating is not a measure of intelligence. See *Cognitive Abilities and the Many Kinds of Smart* in the Appendix for a full explanation.

Case Study: Different Information Processing Speeds

An executive team for a manufacturing firm seemed to be struggling, despite the fact that the team was made up of talented and experienced people being led by an exceptionally-talented and experienced vice president. There was frequent communication between the vice president and the team, but there was a lack of clarity that persisted with five members of his team. BestWork DATA was used to study the relationship of the vice president to those team members. The scale below shows how the team members are distributed on a scale ranging from **processing information slowly** to **processing information quickly.** A gap of a single box requires conscious attention and energy to bridge the gap of understanding caused by the speed difference. The VP was at the highest level of processing speed with two members one gap away, one member two gaps away and two more members three gaps away.

Chart 5. Comparing Information Processing Speed Among Team

Processes Information Slowly		2	1	2	VP	Processes Information Quickly

This was an example of an extremely difficult and almost impossible mismatch between the vice president and half of his team. It is important to understand that all five of the members of the VP's team were well matched to their jobs. Their speed of processing information was exactly right for their jobs. The VP had an exceptional strength that definitely helped him in many ways, but at the same time, it demanded significant effort on his part to communicate effectively with his team members.

Directness of Feedback

Highly assertive managers give extremely direct instruction and feedback. Equally assertive employees expect and need that level of directness. Employees who are less confrontational can be intimidated by that level of directness. In those cases, the assertive managers can unintentionally discourage discussions or new ideas because the less confrontational employees fear the challenges or feedback to their comments.

Case Study: DATA & Team Dynamics

A major athletic shoe company had gone to great lengths to recruit a marketing executive with particular experience in an area of business that was one of their primary targets. Everyone felt that this individual's creativity and knowledge of that market would be of tremendous value. After a year of working with the executive team however, that marketing person had failed to contribute even a single idea or suggestion.

The executive team worked in five-person groups with little structure to their meetings. There was no leader, but rather a free form discussion about the immediate issues. DATA was collected on each of the five team members. The scale showing the level of directness for the members is shown below with M representing the marketing person.

Chart 6. Comparing Level of Directness Among Team

Diplomatic & Non-Confrontational		M			2	2	Direct & Highly Assertive

As in the previous example, a gap of one box is significant. The gaps of two and three boxes between the marketing person and the other four members of the team are gigantic obstacles that preclude any discussion or introduction of new ideas under normal circumstances when the members are already talking. Two simple changes were made. In the meetings, M talked first before the others became engaged in any debates or discussions. Also, prior to the meetings, M provided a quick summary of his current ideas to his boss. Suddenly, they had a flow of the ideas they had expected.

Right Ways, Rules & Procedures

Some people embrace rules, policies and procedures. For them, these provide clarity and direction, freeing them from uncertainty. At the opposite end of the scale, people see those same rules, policies and procedures as limiting their ability to do things in the most efficient and effective way. They view each situation as being different, and for them, each one must be treated differently. When a manager and an employee are on opposite ends of the scale, disagreements occur continually. Each one sees the problem as requiring the very thing that the other one cannot provide.

Case Study: Too Many Rules Spoil the Service

As her responsibilities grew, a successful executive (X) inherited a four-person work group. The range of the group is shown in the next scale in comparison with X.

Chart 7. Comparing Level of Flexibility Among Team

Flexible; Adjusting to Each Situation Differently		2	2			X	Consistent; Following the Rules, Policies & Procedures

The group had been functioning fairly well, using their considerable experience to handle the situations that occurred. The new manager (X) saw that the best way to improve the team was to establish clear rules and procedures for dealing with situations. Consistency was critical from her point of view. Problems multiplied immediately. When the rules did not fit the situation, the group changed the program and solved the problem for the customer as they had always done. The manager saw this as a violation of policy. Rules were then tightened and punishment threatened if they were broken. Now the group had to choose between what they saw as serving the customer in the best way possible or following what they saw as restrictive policies. Quality of service dropped and tension increased.

When DATA revealed what was happening, solutions were obvious. The manager realized that too many rules actually hurt the service by not taking advantage of the problem-solving experience of her team. The team realized that some rules and guidelines actually captured their best practices and made them part of each customer's experience.

Details, Details, Details

Seeing details is a hard-wired strength. These are people who read the fine print, ask the annoying questions and are picky about things other people do not even see. They are often the best accountants, quality control managers, auditors, analysts, nuclear engineers and more. At the other end of the scale however, are wonderful people who probably did not even read all of the big print, asked few questions and are happy as long as nothing obvious is wrong. They make poor accountants, quality control managers, auditors, analysts and do not even think of them being a nuclear engineer.[11]

Chart 8. Comparing Focus on Details Between Candidates

One Page Summary of Highlights		A			B		Multi-Page Narrative With Charts, Graphs and Analysis

We can see this in Chart 8, where the issues arise when the highly detail-oriented manager (B) asks for a report from a less detailed employee (A). The diligent employee puts together a quick one-page summary of highlights which is received by the manager as an example of lazy and incompetent work. The reverse is also a problem. The low-detail manager (A) asks for a report from the highly-detailed employee (B). The multi-page narrative complete with charts, graphs

---

[11] The author, who is woefully oblivious of all details, went to college originally with the dream of being a nuclear engineer. Fortunately, calculus and college physics prevented that disaster.

and analysis is received by the low-detail manager as an example of how little the employee actually understands about the business, having attempted to mask that with volumes of irrelevant details. DATA alerts both the manager and the employee to each other's different expectations and guides them to a practical compromise. See the examples of the *Manage Me* and *My Manager* reports in the Appendix.

Planning vs. Reacting

Two other hard-wired strengths that are important in most businesses are the ability to plan effectively and the ability to react effectively in unplanned situations. Not surprisingly, these strengths are on opposite ends of a single scale. Again, most people share a bit of both, and this serves most circumstances well. It is the extremes of these strengths that offer huge advantages in the right circumstances but create equally troublesome weaknesses in the wrong circumstances.

Chart 9. Comparing Level of Planning Effectively Between Two Baseball Managers

Reacts with Little Need for Planning		A			B		Needs Thorough Planning Before Acting

Case Study: When Do I Play, Coach?

In Chart 9, a minor league baseball player was called up to the majors as a catcher. The manager of that team (A) did

135

little planning for upcoming games, relying instead on his instincts and feelings of the moment. As a result, the catcher (B) never knew when he was going to play in a game until the day of the game. The catcher however, was a player who needed a plan and needed to prepare ahead for a game, both mentally and physically. That season with that team and that manager was one of the catcher's worst years. He never felt right going into a game. He was sent back to the minor leagues, disappointed and believing that his chance was lost. Unexpectedly, he was picked up by another team to fill a spot caused by an injury to one of their catchers. This manager was quite different. He always planned ahead. His lineups were worked out well in advance of the games. The catcher knew days ahead of time when he would play. He could then prepare the way he wanted to. That season he was an All-Star.

Sense of Urgency

A person's sense of urgency depends upon another hard-wired personality trait. The majority of people in the middle of the normal distribution bell curve share similar urgencies with what they do. It is the extreme ends of that scale that introduce some common misunderstandings and frustrations between managers and employees.

Chart 10. Comparing Levels of Urgency Between Two Managers

Relaxed Sense of Urgency; All in Good Time; Patient		A			B		Intense Sense of Urgency; NOW!

The relaxed manager shown in Chart 10 asks the urgent employee to prepare a report. The manager does not need it any time soon, but being relaxed and patient, they assumed the employee would do it whenever they had time. The urgent employee, seeing everything as being urgent, drops whatever they were doing to prepare the report. Upon being given the report, the manager sets it aside and says that he will review over the weekend. The employee is appalled, having set speed records preparing it.

Again, the reverse is no better. The urgent manager tells the relaxed employee that they need the report as soon as possible. The employee places that request in the queue, working patiently through the items in order. The manager, becoming increasingly frustrated as they wait, cannot understand the delay.

In both examples, the manager failed to include a specific deadline for when they needed the report. In the first case, there was no deadline of any kind. Lacking one, the employee's intense sense of urgency supplied what might be called an emotional deadline. In the second example, the manager gave a general deadline, "as soon as possible."

This too, came from his own interpretation with "as soon as possible" meaning right away and ahead of anything else. The employee's relaxed sense of urgency interpreted "as soon as possible" as meaning "whenever you finish the current projects." This is one of the most common causes of frustration between managers and employees. DATA enables both to understand the importance of using specific deadlines rather than the *emotional deadlines* that may be quite different.

The key message in all of these scenarios is that these issues, communication misses, management miscues and outright problems are always happening. They are a part of everyday business life. DATA turns the lights on and enables you to avoid them. Without DATA, they still happen. Without DATA, you have to guess why and what to do.

To Meet or Not to Meet…

About a third of the people in the world get energy from interacting with other people. Another third loses energy when interacting with other people. A manager in the first third loves to meet with his or her team, together and individually. Personal discussions are a primary management tool for them. A manager in the other third finds meetings to be tiring and therefore wants to limit them. Instead theses types of managers rely on email, texts and other indirect communication. It is easy to imagine what happens with mismatches on this scale. The interactive manager looks for opportunities to talk with the reserved employee. In the meetings, the manager wants to encourage discussion, while the employee wants the meeting to end. In the reverse, the interactive employee feels left out or not valued because their time with their manager is so infrequent and limited. With the help of DATA, both parties can usually find a middle ground solution that works. See the examples of the *Manage Me* and *My Manager* reports in the Appendix.

What Role to Play on the Team

All people can be team players; however, there are different roles on any team. Some of those roles fit better than others with each individual's strengths. Some people thrive on individual competition. They are motivated to win, to outperform others and to be the star of the team. Another set of people thrives on supporting the performance of the team, including the stars. They do not want individual recognition and the idea of individual competition is actually demotivating for them. Too often, a manager who is an individual competitor sees that kind of competition as the best motivator for everyone. Consequently, that manager puts in place motivational contests that actually work against his goal. DATA enables you to see the motivational keys for each person. When that is known, it is relatively easy to design programs that work for all.

CHAPTER 13

CAREER PATHS & THEIR DETOURS

Any business can recognize the strengths and abilities of each member of the team using DATA and change or adjust jobs to match to team members.

Trips Along the Career Path

Career paths take many forms. One path may start with an employee position and with solid performance, lead to management roles. Another may start with a low-level management job and move up through a series of management roles with increasing levels of responsibility. Many skills or knowledge-based jobs begin with an apprentice position and then to journeyman and on to a master craftsman. The tricky part is understanding how well the individual's hard-wired strengths and abilities support each stage of the career path. Too often, excellent production workers have been promoted to a supervisory position in which they lacked the necessary strengths to direct the actions of their former fellow workers. Facing failure, these unhappy supervisors left the company and went down the street to another one where they could go back to the job they did well. The story of the top salesperson being promoted to sales manager and then failing in that role is almost a cliché. Many times, the same strengths that were the foundation of success in one job become weaknesses in another one.

In professional baseball, a young athlete may start off as a pitcher in the minor leagues. If his performance continues to improve, he will move up through the minor league levels, but he will remain being a pitcher. If he ultimately reaches the major leagues, he will still be a pitcher. The job did not change, but his skills and capabilities improved with each promotion.

MANY TIMES, THE SAME STRENGTHS THAT WERE THE FOUNDATION OF SUCCESS IN ONE JOB BECOME WEAKNESSES IN ANOTHER ONE.

In the business world, it can be quite different. A person may be promoted from one kind of position into a completely different one. The first job may have required strictly enforcing rules and policies and the next one depends upon creative thinking. One requirement is the opposite of the next. In another case, the first job depends upon reacting to walk-up customers and unexpected situations. The next job demands strong planning and attention to details. Again, the necessary strengths are opposites. Excellent tactical executives are moved into strategic roles in which they struggle.

In large companies, there is often the concept of giving the executive a wide range of experience. Many executive career paths are laid out expressly for that purpose. Unfortunately, the promising executive eventually arrives at a position that is a poor match to their strengths. As a result, their previously impressive performance drops to unacceptable levels. This is foolishly explained as "The Peter Principle." It is nonsense. People can be moved into jobs that are right for them, but the people did not reach a fantasized "level of incompetence." They went down a wrong road. The trip is not abandoned; they just back up and find the right road. People are far too valuable to be discounted with any "Peter Principle" that long ago reached its level of interest or application in the real world.

Example: The Baseball Promotion Parable

A young athlete was drafted onto a professional baseball team which was run in the same way as many businesses with clear career paths. This player was fast on his feet with great hands. He was put on first base where he performed well. On a 10-point scale, his performance was graded 7.

Because he had played well at first base, he was promoted to second base. In that position, he played even better. On first base, he really only moved in one direction. Now on second base, his fast feet could now range in both directions, so he could cover more of the field. On a 10-point scale, it was an 8.

Clearly his performance warranted another promotion. On this team, the next position on the *ladder of success* was catcher. Now his fast feet were useless, crouching behind home plate, with his knees wearing out. His performance took a nose dive. On a 10-point scale it was a 3.

That was not acceptable. The management said that he had lost his motivation or just gone as far as he could. He was traded to another team. Now this team recognized his speed and quickness. They put him at shortstop, the ideal match for those talents. On a 10-point scale it was a 10, and he was an All-Star.

It is important to note that his baseball skills basically stayed the same. The game was definitely the same. The difference was in matching the player's strengths and abilities to the position in which they were most critical.

With DATA, any business can recognize the strengths and abilities of each member of the team. For too long, businesses have thought of people as flexible and jobs as fixed. The wonderful reality is that jobs are flexible and can easily be changed or adjusted. People have clear traits and abilities that can be invaluable in the right job.

CHAPTER 14

WHERE DO THE HIPO's GO?

High potential executives can provide companies with significant future talent, but DATA enables an effective matching of their set of strengths and abilities to particular roles.

The Art of Caring for Your HiPo's

There is a concept that is popular in many companies, by which certain individuals are identified as *high potential executives.* These are executives who are seen to have exceptional potential with respect to filling senior level positions in the company at some point in the future. Identifying future talent is a positive thing. It enables the company to nurture those individuals and encourage their growth through special training opportunities and mentoring programs. The glitch comes in when the *HiPo's* are seen as being equally capable of filling any role. Unfortunately, some *HiPo's* have met the same fate as the baseball player in the previous chapter. They were hand-selected for a key role needing one set of strengths and abilities, with that decision being based on performance in an entirely different role and required an entirely different set of strengths and abilities. *HiPo's* represent a significant investment for the company. When placed properly into roles that match their talents, there are usually significant opportunities for the *HiPo's*. DATA enables both the HiPo's and the company to understand this and to use that information to optimize the decisions for both parties.

Watch for my next book, *Managing with the Lights On*, which will explain more about how DATA can transform performance management for any business.

CHAPTER 15

WHAT CHANGED?

A disruptive innovation introduces a change of such magnitude into an established industry that it disrupts everything in that industry, including performance, quality, pricing, applications and much more.

The mobile phone was disruptive. The personal computer was disruptive. BestWork DATA is disruptive. The interesting thing is that it is impossible to understand the disruptive innovation by comparing it to what it is displacing. The changes are far too great.

> **IMPORTANT NOTE:** BestWork DATA is a disruptive innovation in the assessment industry. This section speaks directly to that disruption. While other parts of the book do mention DATA and its applications, this section is specific in pointing out the advantages of BestWork DATA relative to other options.

What Changed

There is a famous story from the early days of total quality management, contrasting the traditional American view of quality control with that of the Japanese. The Americans were used to discovering the defects during assembly, so when an American firm ordered parts from a Japanese manufacturer, they specified the acceptable percentage of defective parts. Therefore, the purchase order for the parts specified that 5% of the parts would be defective, meaning that as the maximum acceptable number. The Japanese were puzzled by this request, but they complied in their own way. When it arrived, the shipment consisted of two boxes, one large and one small. The small box was clearly labeled as containing the 5% defective parts as ordered. The Japanese could not imagine not knowing which parts were defective at the point of manufacture.

The technology and science of BestWork DATA has a similar effect in a selection process. The accuracy and clarity of the DATA makes it possible to easily identify Bad Hires before hiring them. When that is possible, the concept of interviewing them or even reviewing their resumés is as puzzling as the American company's request for 5% defective parts. Let's explain how such a disruptive innovation came about.

The world of technology and science is moving faster than ever before. The phone you bought a few years ago is now seen as obsolete. The science that you learned in school is not the same, even if you graduated three or four years ago. The assessment industry is unfamiliar to most people. There are over 80,000 occupationally-related products with only a handful based on current science and using the latest technology. If you wish to explore some of the myths, misunderstandings and truths about the world of psychometrics, visit www.aboutassessments.com. This book will explain the major changes that have led to *No Bad Hires*. Some of these changes will be familiar to you, although perhaps not the details. Some will be in conflict with what the salesperson told you when they sold you their tests. You are invited to read this as critically as you wish. The opportunities that it will reveal will be as great as any you have ever found. The objectives we share is to solve your hiring problems and to enhance your business.

THERE ARE OVER 80,000 OCCUPATIONALLY-RELATED PRODUCTS WITH ONLY A HANDFUL BASED ON CURRENT SCIENCE AND USING THE LATEST TECHNOLOGY.

Change #1: The Science of Psychology Moved On

Psychology is an interesting science. It is invisible to most people. Advancements in other sciences make the news. A new type of car engine is announced. A new wonder drug is discovered. The latest airliner is seen at the airport. Meanwhile similar advances and discoveries in psychology pass unnoticed. Over 2,400 years ago, Hippocrates speculated that there were four personality types. He called them: choleric, sanguine, phlegmatic and melancholic. Today, they are more commonly seen as Dominant, Influencing, Steady and Compliant (DISC), or any of the dozens of versions being sold that use that same model. Many companies still use them for simple team building programs. The original word groups and item format for the DISC-type instruments were developed in 1928. Similarly, Myers-Briggs, a product of the 1940s, is commonly found in use within companies that would hesitate to use an older version of software. What is not well known is that serious psychologists have long since abandoned such models for more current theories (see www.aboutassessments.com).

Universal agreement among leading psychologists on what really comprised human personality did not occur until the late 1980s. At that time, a sufficient body of evidence had been accumulated through research, and it was clear that people possessed distinct personality traits that tended to remain stable throughout their lives. The good news was that these traits could be measured. The measurements could then be compared to those of other people or to certain traits related to job behaviors. Instruments based on the Big Five Personality Factors, the model accepted in the psychological world, offered a depth and specificity of data that was far beyond earlier personality models, such as DISC and Myers-Briggs. Virtually all quality instruments developed in the last 20 years have been based on the Big Five Model. The construct for BestWork DATA's personality instrument isolated those elements of the Big Five that are most relevant to the business world. The result was that the DATA was more focused on specific job behaviors rather than generalized personality descriptions.

Change #2: Quicker, Easier, Kind of Fun and More Accurate, Too

Traditionally, the paradox of assessment instruments has been that the ones that were quick and easy to use, using adjective checklists or word choices, produced fairly limited information based on simple models. The quality instruments that produced more specific and reliable information were long, somewhat tedious and not a pleasant experience. In the half century that has passed since many of these products were created, psychometric science has also moved forward. The item formats today are much more refined. The importance of the user experience has become part of the design. The items in BestWork DATA's personality survey capture extraordinary DATA that is more robust than that of the classic ones that took three or four times as long. The item design also produces a positive experience for the participants.

Change #3: Better Computers, Better DATA

Advances in computer technology have generated parallel advances in the business applications of psychometric science. As late as 1993, a major assessment product bragged about being developed with unlimited mainframe computer time. In 1993, this was meaningful. Unlimited computer time meant deeper statistical analysis being available as the instrument was being developed and consequently, more accurate results. This book is being written on an Apple laptop with more power than that mainframe in 1993. Psychometric instruments developed in the last 10 years benefited from a level of computer technology unimaginable in the 80's and 90's. Deeper analysis means greater accuracy. It means more reliable measurement. Just as an MRI produces images not possible with X-rays, BestWork DATA produces information not available using earlier tools.

Change #4: Knowledgework or Routine; Cognitive Abilities Are Key

Technology has accelerated the lifecycle of jobs. Thousands of jobs have vanished, thousands of new jobs have been created and the jobs that exist continue to change and evolve at a faster pace than ever before. Traditional assessment companies once collected huge libraries of job profiles. Today, these are obsolete. Even when the jobs still exist, they are rarely the same within different companies.

Jobs that used to be simple have now become complex. Knowledgework has become critical to many jobs. Without any measure of a candidate's cognitive abilities, it is impossible to know whether or not they can do the job, and whether or not any specialized training will be effective.

At the same time, service jobs have multiplied dramatically. Many of these jobs depend upon fundamentally routine tasks delivered over and over again, day after day. The ability to handle that routine is absolutely dependent on cognitive abilities. Candidates lacking those abilities are usually quick to turnover in those jobs.

While cognitive ability's critical importance to job performance actually predates that awareness with personality, the instruments used for measuring it have been either rudimentary or frustratingly complicated. BestWork DATA has the most sophisticated and advanced cognitive instrument in the industry. DATA is available that matches and even exceeds the accuracy and reliability of instruments requiring almost an hour. More importantly, the DATA is designed to work with all ranges of jobs, from complex roles to the simplest of routines.

Change #5: No Experts, Special Training or Profiling Needed

Over the last 20 years, there have been several excellent assessment products in the market with good data. Using these products required an expert to interpret the data or specialized training and certification for others to do so. This severely limited the use of the information. Often the consulting fees were many times greater than the cost of the tests.

One solution was to use the old profiling methodology. "Top performers" were selected, usually a questionable process at best, and those were assessed to create a template or profile that could be used to compare job candidates. This method produced a percentage of how well the candidate's scores matched the profile. Scores above a certain range were supposed to indicate a good hire. The concept was sound and almost right. Too often high scoring candidates failed. One excellent test showed a sales candidate to be a 92% match to the profile of "top salespeople." Unfortunately, the missing 8% was the ability to persuade prospects to make buying decisions. This became worse as the changes in jobs and the markets accelerated, making even good profiles outdated.

BestWork DATA requires no experts and no special training. It is immediately understandable by anyone and is specific to any job. There is never a need for profiling. The focus is always on the individual's ability to perform the critical job behaviors that are necessary for success in that specific position. There are hundreds of existing job reports, and a user can easily customize their own in a matter of minutes using BestWork DATA's JobSmith™ program. Job reports can also be modified at any time when the job requirements change.

Change #6: Pricing in a Digital World - Cents Not Dollars

Pricing has been a major limiting factor in the use of good assessments. At one time, test companies mailed out test booklets to customers. Customers had job candidates fill in the booklets, and then their answers were sent to the test company, where they were interpreted. The results were then sent back to the customer. Of course, all of this has changed. Nothing is mailed and everything is online. Computer programs provide the interpretation and are all digital. Unfortunately, the pricing for many products has never reflected the change to digital costs. Some of the classic assessments sell for $150 per use or more. Prices of over $250 per use are not uncommon. Even simple tools are often $25 per use or more.

BestWork DATA is absolutely a digital product. It is priced accordingly. It is sold as an unlimited usage annual license based on the number of existing employees. The unlimited usage enables clients to not only inventory the strengths of their existing employees but to use the DATA with 100% of their applicants. BestWork DATA reports are available for almost any decision point in the lifecycle of an employee. The license enables a client to access a menu of these reports at any time.

Change #7: It Is No Longer Just for Executives

Hiring has become much more complex. In the past, companies that used assessments, only used them with important higher level executive positions and salespeople. Now, even mid- or low-level employees have considerable responsibility and can contribute to the success or failure of the company. Any position that is customer-facing, involving an employee having direct contact with customers, is critical. The effect of an unsatisfactory customer experience can be multiplied a thousand times with today's social media. In many industries, people are the only competitive advantage, with consumers seeking a more personal buying experience. It is not enough to be simply efficient and competent. It is not enough to have excellent products or services. The customer experience has become paramount for every company competing for business. It has become imperative for competitive companies to know not only that a candidate CAN do the job but also HOW they will do the job.

BestWork DATA's pricing structure allows any company to use DATA for all positions. The wide range of jobs and the ability of JobSmith™ to produce reports for any type of position enables BestWork users to adapt the reports to any special needs. The specific job behavior descriptions give recruiters a clear picture of HOW each element of a job will be performed. This is a degree of control that has not previously been available.

Change #8: Where Did All of Those Resumés Come From?

The Internet has made it incredibly easy for job seekers to send out resumés to any job posting in which they have the least interest. One client received 225 resumés for an executive assistant position. A sales manager received 214 resumés for a sales position in the first three hours after it was posted. A call center with 40 openings received over 8,000 resumés from candidates interested in those positions. Just giving quick reviews to each resumé is a daunting task, without even considering how effective such a review would be. BestWork DATA offers a quick screening feature that filters out those candidates that lack the critical strengths necessary to perform certain jobs. This screening process usually eliminates at least half of the initial flood of resumés and often even more. This not only makes the task more reasonable, but at the same time, it facilitates the selection with additional information and even provides interview questions for those candidates that have moved forward in the process. This allows talented personnel specialists and recruiters to focus their attention on selecting the best candidates from a pool of pre-screened candidates.

> **IMPORTANT NOTE:** There are now online services that promise to deliver "qualified candidates" to companies that are tired of reading resumés and scheduling interviews. These services screen the candidates based on the skills, experience and education elements of the circles. While this is more efficient in terms of sourcing candidates, it does not ensure good candidates. It is easy to insert BestWork DATA into that process, which does ensure that each candidate not only has the skill, experience and education needed, but that they also have the job behaviors needed to be successful in the job.

Change #9: From Hiring to Talent Management

As jobs have become more complex and hiring more challenging, companies have discovered that the actual hiring of a new employee is only the first step toward realizing the benefits of their talents and abilities. Incorporating their talents and abilities into the company's operation involves a series of stages and many different people, and at each stage, how the new employee is handled affects their overall and long range value to the company. The onboarding process is different for each person. Some people find a desk and get straight to work, while others need to meet each of their coworkers, understand the complete network of procedures in their area and become comfortable in that understanding before beginning to tackle the new job. BestWork DATA offers an Onboarding Keys report that explains the most effective way to onboard each new hire.

People also participate in training differently, according to their strengths and abilities. Some people breeze through training, asking few questions and needing little support. Others, equally talented, learn more deliberately, ask a lot of questions and need some initial support to feel comfortable. Knowing these differences allows the company to meet each new employee's needs, and at the same time, bring them up to an acceptable level of productivity in the shortest period of time. BestWork DATA's menu includes a Training Coach report, which advises trainers on the individual training needs of each person.

Managers are busy people. Their ability to take time to really learn about new employees is limited. Those first few weeks are generally a honeymoon period with the new employee doing everything to look good and with the manager supplying a higher level of support and forgiving early mistakes. When the manager knows the key issues of managing a new employee at Day One, they can be proactive in their management, getting everyone off to a faster start. BestWork DATA gives the manager a Manage Me report for each new hire, calling out the key issues that are important for each new employee.

It is not only the manager who needs information on this new relationship. BestWork DATA's My Manager report uses the manager's DATA to coach the new employee on how to work most effectively with their new manager.

Change #10: The Speed of Business Is Too Fast For That

Computer technology and the Internet have increased the speed of business in virtually every industry. Decisions must be made more quickly. Problems occur faster. Competition evolves faster. More things come and they come more quickly. Old methods of evaluating job candidates move far too slowly in today's world. Selection systems must be able to drive quicker decisions with less risk, enabling businesses to capture top talent. Talent pools vary according to the type of job, the location and other factors, but in general, the following rules apply:

- If your selection process takes over two weeks, you are selecting from B and C candidates. The A's were snapped up in the first week or the second.

- If your selection process takes over four weeks, you are picking over C candidates. The A's and the B's are gone.

BestWork DATA's ability to screen out Bad Hires immediately collapses your time to decision. Then the DATA helps you to identify the best candidates of those remaining. This allows you to expedite the process with the ones that are most desirable.

The dynamic nature of BestWork DATA enables clients to evaluate candidates for any type of job, even positions that may not be posted. A candidate may have responded to a posting for one position and not be a good match for that job, but the DATA can show the company that are quite right for another job. This capability gives the employer more scope in their recruiting efforts.

When the jobs change, as they must, the systems must be dynamic, changing just as fast. BestWork DATA system easily adapts to changes in jobs and to new situations, without the need for building new profiles or bringing in consultants.

CHAPTER 16

CASE STUDIES USING DATA

During the past eight years, BestWork DATA has been developed and proven in the business world with hundreds of clients and hundreds of thousands of participants. These engagements have led to the creation of a DATA-based human capital management system with applications for any business element that depends on the performance of people.

BestWork DATA Case Studies

Case Study #1: Sales – Product Sales vs. Solution Sales

A Fortune 100 company had historically provided technical products to a wide range of manufacturing industries. When factories expanded, they would order more products as needed. When new products were added or others updated, the company's salespeople would call the factories and take orders for what was needed. As the world of technology became more global, many small offshore companies sprang up offering competing products at lower prices. After watching their core business being eroded in this way, the Fortune 100 giant reasoned that while small companies may each offer a few of its products, none could provide a total solution such as they could. This called for a strategic change in their sales force. Now they would sell solutions. The salespeople would engage the customers, learn their business, identify the various opportunities and craft a solution integrating all of the possibilities into one proposal.

A major sales training organization was retained to teach solution selling to the existing sales force at a cost of $1.2 million. That year the sales force attained only 47% of their sales goal. A second prominent sales training organization was retained to further train the existing sales team on how to sell solutions at a similar cost to the first group. That year, the sales team reached 52% of their goal.

At that point, someone suggested inventorying the strengths and abilities of the sales team before engaging any other training initiatives. The resulting DATA is shown in Chart 11 below.

Chart 11. Distribution of Strengths on the Sales Team

Job Behavior							Job Behavior
CAN HANDLE A SIMPLE SALES PROCESS	2	16	19	45	31	7	CAN HANDLE A COMPLEX SALES PROCESS
SELLS STANDARDIZED PRODUCTS	15	30	24	27	20	4	SELLS CUSTOMIZED SOLUTIONS

IDEAL FOR PRODUCT SALES

OKAY FOR PRODUCT SALES

All 120 of the salespeople were ideally or acceptably suited for handling a simple sales process, which was what they had done successfully for years. All 120 of the salespeople were either ideally or acceptably suited for selling standardized products, such as they

167

had historically done. Essentially, the company had an outstanding team for the sales process that no longer existed. The question was how well they matched what was needed now. Instead of a simple sales process, it was now a complex sales process.

Instead of selling standardized products, it was now selling customized solutions. When the DATA of the sales force was compared to those job behaviors in Chart 12, the problem became crystal clear.

Chart 12. Distribution of Strengths on the Sales Team

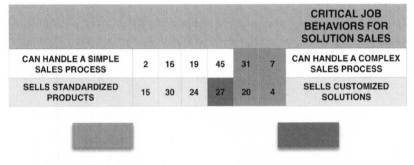

Only 32% of the sales team had the ability to handle a complex sales process such as the one introduced to this team. Only 42% of them had the ability to sell customized solutions. At best, less than half the team had a reasonable chance to succeed with the new sales program. If it was a baseball team, at least five players would have no gloves in the field and no bats to use at the plate. No amount of training or coaching could make up for that. **Good hires who were top**

performers in one type of sale were changed into bad hires for a very different type of sale.

The Solution: Now that it was clear that training was not going to solve the problem, triage for the situation became critical. First, three teams were set up with salespeople who did have the key strengths and abilities. Next, existing customers and prospective customers were sorted into A's, B's and C's, according to their revenue potential. A's were immediately visited to ensure that their needs and issues were understood and under control. Next, B's and lastly, C's were evaluated and handled in the same way. Recruiters were given DATA-defined parameters to use as new additions to the sales team were added. The existing sales team members that did not fit the solution were redirected into their former roles or similar jobs that did fit their abilities. Within a year, sales were headed in the right direction to achieve the goals of the organization.

Case Study #2: Customer Service Call Center – Cool to Friendly
A call center took inbound calls from customers having a problem or with a question about their products. Time and again, the call center received excellent reviews on the quality of their service and their ability to resolve problems quickly. The only negative comments described the agents as "impersonal" or "not particularly friendly." BestWork DATA was used to inventory the strengths of the call center. Half of the people in the world tend to be quieter than the other half. They show less enthusiasm and project less energy on a phone

call, resulting in the call feeling somewhat impersonal to the customer. The other half cannot stop being enthusiastic, warm and friendly on a call. The inventory showed that about 68% of the agents in the call center were on the quiet and impersonal side of the scale. Once the DATA showed the cause, the solution was simple.

The Solution: The recruiters were asked to select only those job candidates with the strengths for being warm and friendly. As normal attrition took place, agents were replaced with those candidates. After about six months, the percentage had shifted with 60+% of the agents being on the warm and friendly side of the scale. Customer reviews began to comment on how much friendlier the agents were.

Without DATA, the traditional solution for this situation would have been a training program on being friendlier with customers. For the 68% of agents that were wired to be impersonal, it would have been like a class on being tall for short people, hoping to improve their basketball game.

Case Study #3: Call Center – Training for Turnover

A group of call centers believed that training was the key to excellent customer service. They recruited agents for the centers and prior to hiring, put them into a two-day intensive training program after which they were given a test. If they passed the test, then they were hired.

Unfortunately, the turnover in the centers was horrendous, with most new hires leaving within 90 days or less. The centers paid well and managers were positive and understanding, but still the turnover persisted. It was time for a DATA-based perspective on the problem. After a strengths and ability inventory of the agents in the call centers, and a job behavior look at the agents' actual job, there was a clear anomaly in the training/job relationship. The training program was quite intense, with considerable information and procedures being presented in a relatively short period of time. In fact, to be successful in passing the test required a faster than average speed of learning. Therefore, virtually all of the candidates being hired after passing the test were fast learners. The job, however, was incredibly routine. Agents answered inbound calls whenever a customer was out of a simple product, and then the agent would enter an order for restocking that product. This was the total job, call after call, day after day. The fast learners were bored before the end of the first day. How long they stayed depended mainly on how long it took them to find another job.

The Solution: DATA-driven reports that could be easily understood by the recruiters were used to select candidates that could handle extended routine. The training program was extended, and regular refresher classes were added. The overall result was a 30% - 40% decrease in turnover across the centers.

Case Study #4: From Rock Star to GOAT or Misplacing a Good Manager

A major pharmaceutical company was heavily invested in a particular state, and that state had recently changed its regulations which affected drug purchases within major hospitals. That change meant that more aggressive salespeople were needed who could deal with a more complex sales process. A strong team was assembled, and to ensure their success, a long time senior executive with a long record of success in all of his previous positions was transferred in to take charge. After six months, the team was a disaster with no apparent leadership and everyone was complaining, the team about the manager and the manager about the team. Consultants were brought in, but before they began, DATA on the team and the manager was collected. The distribution of the salespeople along with the manager (M) is shown below on Chart 13.

Chart 13. Manager (M) & Distribution of the New Team (15 members)

Slower information processing			M	7	8	Fast information processing
Avoids confrontation and debate			M	10	5	Direct & confrontational in debating ideas
Looks for innovative solutions and change	5	9	1		M	Conventional and traditional thinker
Private & reserved		M		4	11	Enthusiastic & outgoing

It would be difficult to have engineered a worse match. The team processed ideas quickly, debated them, favored innovation and did all of this with high energy and interaction. The manager could not keep up with their speed of processing, was put off by their open debates and direct discussions, was hesitant or against change or new ideas and tended to be quiet and reserved in the meetings. The team described him as hardly even being there. The manager described the team as out of control. The important thing to note is that no one was doing anything wrong. The manager and the team were both doing what they did well. It was the match that was wrong.

The Solution: The obvious question is how in the world did this manager have such a glowing record of success in his previous roles. The chart below shows his previous team.

Chart 14. Manager (M) & Distribution of the Original Team (12 members)

Slower information processing	8	4	M			Fast information processing
Avoids confrontation and debate	3	6	3 & M			Direct & confrontational in debating ideas
Looks for innovative solutions and change				7	5 & M	Conventional and traditional thinker
Private & reserved	4	4 & M	4			Enthusiastic & outgoing

They were not salespeople. They were pharmaceutical research scientists. He processed information faster than that team. These were some of the leading scientists in their field, but the research extended over a decade or more. Fast processors could never do that. The scientists were completely non-confrontational. The manager could easily manage them. Few things are as rigidly defined as the drug industry, so his conventional thinking was perfect. All of the scientists tended to be equally reserved and private. This was an excellent match for the manager. DATA saved his career and showed where he was best suited to lead.

Everyone is right for some jobs. No one is right for all jobs. No matter what your strengths and abilities are, in the wrong job, the most that you can hope for is to be adequate. You will not excel. In the right job, you will almost always prosper.

Case Study #5: Low Turnover in Historically High Turnover Jobs
One of the toughest jobs to fill is found in the pest control industry. Throughout the industry, the job of pest control technician, the person who sprays the bug spray in the customers' homes and businesses, has a turnover rate of over 100%. It is a challenging job for most people.

The Solution: A large regional company used BestWork DATA to understand the critical job behaviors in that job and the cognitive and personality factors that caused turnover. After two years of refining that model, turnover in that job has dropped to 10%, but 5% of that is produced by promotions from that job into supervisory roles.

Case Study #6: Faster Sales in a Car Dealership
Car dealerships typically struggle to find successful car salespeople. Far too often, the decisions are made by sales managers who are short on time for interviewing and who need to focus on closing deals with their current salespeople. They are often short-handed, and there is a pressure to simply fill the openings. Rarely does this type of hiring

pay off. Dealerships spend huge sums of money on advertising and marketing, simply to get customers to come to the car lot. Bad Hires can only offer these customers an unhappy experience, producing neither sales nor smiles.

The Solution: DATA presents a vastly different opportunity for dealerships. A large dealer for one of the major brands, like most others, hired its salespeople primarily through interviews by the sales manager. In fact, the majority of his time was spent in this manner. This was the principal reason that he decided to use DATA to screen out applicants who were not going to be able to sell cars prior to any interviewing by him. To his surprise, this process screened out almost 60% of the applicants. While this accomplished his primary objective, the bigger surprise came from the sales results of the hires made using DATA. Historically, it took about six weeks before a new salesperson sold a car. The salespeople hired with DATA were selling cars within two weeks. Eliminating Bad Hires at the beginning of the selection process not only enabled the company to capture car-selling talent more efficiently, but the normal standards of sales performance were completely changed.

Case Study #7: Talented but Unreliable IT Team

A university had a 19-person IT team, providing support and services to the various departments of the institution. Each member of the IT team had been tested on their IT skills and knowledge. Each one had been required to demonstrate those skills and knowledge prior to being hired. Each one was rock-solid in those areas. Despite this, the IT department was universally regarded as unreliable. BestWork DATA was used to essentially *inventory* the strengths of the 19 team members. Chart 15 below shows the distribution of the team members in terms of how consistent they were with standards and procedures.

Chart 15. IT Manager (*) & the Distribution of IT Team (18 members)

LOOSE STANDARDS & PROCEDURES	2	6*	8	3			CONSISTENT STANDARDS & PROCEDURES

Sixteen members of the team favored loose standards and tended to adapt procedures to whatever was happening. In other words, there was no standard response time to service calls. There was no standard procedure for prioritizing calls. It was like a football team made up of talented athletes without any set plays or strategies. The asterisk indicated the head of the IT department. Without using any DATA, he was doing his very best to select team members, and in his interviews, he was unconsciously drawn to candidates just like himself.

The Solution: Once the source of the problem was understood, a set of performance standards was put into place. It is important to understand that this would not work by itself. Those individuals who are wired to be flexible and loose with standards can usually find a reason to make exceptions to the standards. The compliance with the standards required close monitoring and tracking. No one was terminated, but with the tightening of the procedures and the monitoring, it became uncomfortable for some of those favoring a looser workplace. As the attrition occurred, DATA enabled the recruiters to bring in equally-skilled IT technicians but ones which enjoyed more structure.

Case Study #8: Which President?

A holding company was searching for two presidents for two of their companies. One was a 50-year-old old manufacturer of basic office products. It was profitable and stable in a rock solid market, and the board wanted that to continue. The second company was faced with dramatic challenges as their world of paper-based forms embraced digital technology. After decades of profitability, it was now a turnaround in crisis.

The Solution: DATA was used to select each of the presidents, and each was successful in their respective roles. It is insightful to compare how the unique strengths and abilities of each were matched to the different needs of the two companies.

Chart 16. President A (Continuing Operations) & President B (Total Turnaround)

Uncomfortable with Confrontation			A	B	Can Handle Higher Levels of Confrontation

The manufacturing operation had been operating smoothly for decades and was expected to continue that way. The new president (A) would face little or no challenges in the transition. The turnaround demanded the layoff of more than half of the employees, the complete retooling of their plant and the shift to a completely different type of business. This would entail endless confrontations, debates and negotiations for the new president (B).

The new president of the manufacturing operation (A) was charged with continuing the historic success of that business, which meant not changing what had always worked. In contrast, almost everything was changing in the turnaround and that president (B) was the primary agent of those changes.

Chart 17. President A (Continuing Operations) & President B (Total Turnaround)

Extreme Change	B		A	Consistency; Minimal Change

The manufacturing business was stable with few problems. President (A) could focus on tactical things such as quality, profitability and customer service. The turnaround would have a myriad of unexpected problems, and every decision had strategic importance. President (B) needed very different strengths to do this.

Chart 18. President A (Continuing Operations) & President B (Total Turnaround)

Tactical Focus; Few Problems		A		B	Strategic Focus; Fast Problem Solver

Case Study #9: Customer Relationships or Sales? Pick One

A printing industry association had sponsored a number of sales training programs for its members. These sales programs had emphasized the importance of building relationships with the customers as the cornerstone of success sales. The member companies had embraced this thinking in their sales strategies and how they managed their sales teams. Hiring interviews focused on identifying those candidates who would be better at building such relationships. The only problem was that the overall sales results remained stagnant and even dropped in some cases. This was a case of a generalized concept that contains an element of truth being taken as a guiding principle without examining what other variables might impact the situation.

With the exception of most retail sales, selling depends upon some level of persuasion. Professional salespeople move their prospects to make a series of buying decisions, such as:

- Defining a specific objective or quality that is desired.
- Specifying a time frame for decisions.
- Naming a budget for the purchase.
- Identifying the decision making process.

These decisions are collectively referred to as *closing the sale*. This is not one major event, but a series of small persuasive elements addressing the questions, objections and stalls of the prospect. Half of the people in the world cannot do this. The ability to do that is absolutely dependent upon a single hard-wired personality trait.

A separate issue is that of building a relationship with prospects. Individuals who enjoy interacting with other people are obviously more likely to build a relationship. The catch occurs in how that person views and participates in competition. About one third of the population values the relationship more than the sale. Another third values the sale ahead of the relationship. The vast majority of top salespeople fall into the second category. For them, the sale is the basis of the relationship. The other group does not want the sale to interfere with or affect the relationship. The relationship-favoring group tend to offer the best deals to their customers along with various extras.

The Solution: DATA was utilized to uncover that the problems with the majority of the printing salespeople in the study were of two types. The first type included salespeople who could close sales but were relationship-focused. The profit margins of their deals were the lowest in the group. The second group was also relationship-focused but could not close sales. They made many friends but few customers.

BestWork DATA enables you to see exactly how a sales candidate will approach selling if you hire them. It is possible to build customer relationships, but that objective must be secondary to creating customers through a sale.

Case Study #10: Tall-Short Jobs

Most jobs were created without considering how hard-wired strengths and abilities both support and limit various job behaviors. Consequently, it is not uncommon to discover what are called *Tall-Short Jobs*. Those are jobs that require two completely opposite sets of strengths. For example, a major accounting firm had a position in its global marketing department with the responsibility for directing the graphic arts team (call it the *Tall* part of the job). That same individual was also responsible for securing approval signatures from any partner authorizing changes to a marketing project (call this the *Short* part of the job). Partners were notorious for avoiding this, and it required extreme tenacity and a hard tolerance for confrontation to get the signatures. For years, many people were hired for that job. Some got signatures but ran off too many talented artists. Others managed the artists brilliantly but could not get the necessary signatures. The firm assumed this was a tough job and raised the salary accordingly. That simply made it a high paying *Tall-Short Job*.

DATA showed the job behaviors needed to manage artists required a level of sensitivity that made the confrontation to get the signatures impossible. The level of emotional toughness and directness needed to get the signatures made it impossible to recognize or deliver the sensitive feedback needed by the artists. There were two distinctly different job crammed into one. Once that was seen, it became easy to fill those roles.

Case Study #11: IT Developers Are Not All the Same

When jobs demand a certain set of skills or knowledge, those skills or knowledge become a primary decision point in a selection process. **Yes** if they have them; **No** if they do not. Too often, the hiring decision is made at that point.

Two software companies in Silicon Valley actively recruited the IT talent specializing in the same programming language. While each company tested the proficiency of each candidate to confirm their skills, each experienced unexplained turnover in those positions.

There is a hard-wired personality trait that determines the degree to which a person prefers to work alone or to work with others. Those that wish to work alone, gain energy when working alone and lose energy when working with other people. Conversely, those that wish to work with others, gain energy from working with others and lose energy when working alone. This is what caused the turnover in both companies.

The Solution: DATA was used to analyze candidates regarding this trait. One company prided itself on providing a private office for each developer, promising to give them plenty of space to work without being bothered by other people. The other company prided itself on providing a collaborative work environment with open work spaces surrounding a community working area. DATA easily unlocked the mystery and enabled each company to hire exactly the kind of developers it wanted.

95% OF HR PROFESSIONALS SAY THAT HAVING PREDICTIVE ANALYTICS WOULD HELP THEM HIRE AND DEVELOP BETTER EMPLOYEES.

CHAPTER 17

HIRING MYTHS & DATA REALITIES

Falling for hiring myths can lead to Bad Hires. DATA can shine the light on many hiring realities and make your business decisions exponentially more effective.

After 25 years of experience using DATA with hundreds of clients and thousands of individuals, there are some clear realities that have been proven time and again. Understanding these realities can help you to use DATA more effectively in your business decisions.

"Smarts" and Degrees Cannot Overcome a Lack of Critical Strengths

Having a degree from Harvard, MIT or the local community college cannot compensate for the lack of the critical strengths or abilities necessary to perform a particular job. An MBA does not ensure that the candidate can actually manage other people or the operations of a business. Only DATA can accurately answer that question. If the necessary strengths and abilities are there, those degrees can be powerful compliments.

"Smart" Salespeople May Not Close Sales

A "smart" salesperson who is hard-wired to avoid confrontation cannot close sales. They may understand the product or service completely, even better than anyone else. They may be friendly and engaging, able to deliver enthusiastic presentations. The only missing part is the ability to move prospects to make buying decisions. They may be effective in other roles within the sales process, as the subject matter expert or supporting a sales team member who can persuade prospects to make decisions. This kind of team sales effort can be extremely effective with many complex technology sales.

"Smart" Is Not Good for All Jobs

In fact, "smart" is disastrous for many jobs. Jobs that depend upon routine or repetitive tasks become turnover engines with "smart" hires.

Marketing Degrees Do Not Always Come With Creativity

Individuals have a range of creativity that is determined first by their personality traits and cognitive abilities. Their skills and experience in expressing their creativity is next in importance. The third part is their palette, the vocabulary of art and ideas that they have explored which gives them food and intellectual materials for their own work. DATA can measure the scope of what they can do with that creativity. Is it focused on a narrow range of rethinking what already exists? Is it off into totally new worlds of imagination? All people are creative, but in vastly different ways. DATA can help match candidates to type of creative work you need.

Selling Is More Than Telling Great Stories

Most people know someone who is a magnificent story teller. They are the life of the party and tell the best jokes. Someone always characterizes that individual as being a "born salesperson". The ability to speak with enthusiasm and easily meet people seems to be a natural fit with the job of selling. Those are indeed beneficial to a salesperson, and for some types of sales, they are critical strengths. However, there are other critical strengths that are equally important, and without them, sales success is almost impossible. The ability to be persuasive is essential. Salespeople must deal with confrontation in handling the objections of customers. Some sales require an exceptionally high speed of learning and information processing. DATA helps to see if the story teller can also close sales and what kind of sales are best for them.

Great Interviewees Are Not Always Great Candidates

Interviews are important to a selection process, but not in the way that many businesses see them. The personal contact of an interview is more real than the resumé, and this causes it to carry more weight in the decision than it probably deserves. What you actually know after a great interview is that the candidate is a great interviewee. If you are hiring interviewees, then you have an excellent first hand demonstration of how well this individual performs the role of interviewee. Of course, there are intangibles that you may draw from the experience. You may "like" the candidate and see them as a "fit" with the company culture. This is definitely information that should go into your evaluation, but great interviewees create that feeling with the interviewers naturally and can enhance that effect with practice and training. DATA gives you an objective picture of the candidate's true capabilities with regard to how they will actually perform in specific jobs.

Success Does Not Always Travel Well

A common mistake in hiring is that of believing that success in a particular job in one company automatically translates into success in a similar job in another company. Certainly, the experience gained in one place can be valuable in any subsequent position. It is the job behaviors that can be significantly different. It can often be as dramatic as asking a great baseball player to switch to ice hockey, expecting his superior athletic ability to translate into success in a very different sport. BestWork DATA unbundles the job titles and responsibilities into specific elements of job behavior that can easily be compared to the needs of the particular position and circumstances.

Friends & Relatives May Not Be Your Best Source of Talent

Well-meaning friends and relatives may suggest one of their friends and relatives as a potential job candidate for you. While it is possible that they are the talent you have been seeking, it is important for you to use DATA to confirm that possibility. Having a consistent screening and selection process for all candidates helps you avoid being in an awkward decision spot.

Recruiters Handle the Screening & Selection

The goal of most recruiters is to present you with a number of candidates that they feel match your needs. These candidates usually have the particular skills or experience that you have requested. Rarely are the candidates screened with tools as advanced or as thorough as BestWork DATA. Many clients now apply that screening to the recruiters' candidates, accepting only those that pass that screen.

APPENDIX

- FAQ's
- Legal Issues
- Background Checks & Special Testing – Drug, Honesty, Skills Testing & More
- References – Giving and Receiving
- Demonstration & Inbox Exercises
- Values & Interest Surveys – Looking for Intangibles
- The Myth and Misses of Profiling
- Cognitive Abilities and the Many Kinds of Smart
- Report Samples – *Manage Me* and *My Manager*

FAQ's

These are some of the most common questions about using assessments. The disruptive nature of BestWork DATA eliminates many of the concerns and challenges in the use of traditional products, and it introduces opportunities that did not exist before. If you have questions that are not answered here, visit the website www.nobadhires.com.

We have had good results with another product that we have used for years. Why should we change?

My guess is that you were delighted with your original cell phone, but having experienced the features that are available with newer ones, you probably changed. In a technology-driven world, better DATA enables you to make better decisions. Today those better decisions may be a competitive advantage. Tomorrow you may need better DATA to stay competitive. In a year or so, you will need that level of DATA to stay in business. Besides, you can try it for free with the link in the book.

We use recruiters to find our candidates. Their job is to find good people. Why should we use testing?

Recruiters face the same challenges as any employer when looking for good candidates. DATA enables them to see Bad Hires before sending them to you for interviews. That helps you but causes them to need more candidates, as DATA will screen out some that previously would have been sent to you. With the fees paid for talented recruiters, you can ensure their success by using DATA.

Our selection process is too long already. Adding testing to it is too much, isn't it?

Used properly, BestWork DATA can actually collapse the time needed for your selection process. First, if you are dealing with a high volume of resumés, BestWork DATA can automatically screen out those candidates that lack the critical strengths needed to perform the job in question. Next, the DATA enables you to have confidence in the candidate's abilities, so that if the first interview is satisfactory, the selection process can be accelerated. For situations in which talent is in high demand, DATA gives you the confidence to make an early contingency offer. This allows you to capture talent more efficiently than your competitors.

Is testing legal?

Absolutely! In fact, the use of normative tools, such as BestWork DATA, is the only way to document nondiscriminatory hiring practices. The instruments have been proven to be blind to race, sex, age, education, ethnic origin or other factors. The same is not true for interviews.

Won't some people be offended when asked to complete the test?

There will always be a few people who react in that way. Those are people you do not want to hire. They balked at the very first thing you asked them to do. What other things do you think will "offend" them once you have started paying them a salary? It is important to understand that the way each candidate handles each aspect of your selection process tells something about them. When a candidate balks at providing you key information for your hiring decision, that action is itself a loud and clear message about how well they will fit on your team.

Are there people who don't do well on tests?

First, it is important to understand what is meant by "well". BestWork DATA enables the participants to accurately describe themselves as to how they learn, process information, make decisions, interact with others and much more. If their behaviors are a good match for the behaviors needed in a particular job, it could be described as "doing well". On the other hand, if their behaviors are a poor match with the behaviors needed in that particular job, the results are also positive because they keep that participant from taking a job in which they would not do "well". This also keeps the employer from making a Bad Hire.

To answer the question in a more technical way, it is rare for the timed section of BestWork DATA to be fully completed by any participant. Some participants complete only a few of the questions. There is no poor score. There is no better score. Completing almost all of the items is a knockout score for some jobs in which that cognitive ability would be counterproductive in that job. Completing only a few of the questions might indicate an excellent match for certain jobs.

One of the wonderful advantages of using BestWork DATA is that it enables people to see themselves through their strengths rather than their weaknesses.

We use a customized interview program. How does testing fit into that?

The difficulty with any interview program is that it ultimately depends upon interviewers with varying skills, perspectives and objectives to make accurate assessments of a candidate's capabilities, which can now be easily and reliably measured by BestWork DATA in about 25 minutes. This eliminates spending time with unsuitable candidates by screening out those that do not have the critical factors needed for a particular job. BestWork DATA then provides behavioral event-based interview questions that target the specific issues for each individual candidate. Adding questions about work experience and other elements to this foundation creates a powerful interview program that is customized at the individual level.

We use an industrial psychologist. Why would we use testing?

A client was using an excellent psychologist to evaluate executive hires. The candidates took a battery of tests and the psychologist produced a report which summarized the results. The company typically used this process for about one hundred candidates each year at a cost of $1,000 per candidate. BestWork DATA replaced that process with customized reports for all positions in the company, including training, managing, onboarding and team engineering reports. For about 20% of the cost of testing 100 candidates, the company now used a much more comprehensive and user-friendly program with over 2,000 employees and thousands of job candidates. If any additional services were needed for certain candidates, the psychologist could be added.

What about building our own test, just for our company?

First of all, done correctly, that is an extremely expensive project. It is fraught with all manner of statistical issues with the population within the company being used for the validation studies. Easy to use products, such as BestWork DATA, already exist and are proven to be accurate and reliable. They are inexpensive and come with a broad menu of applications.

We want a candidate that fits our culture. How can testing help?

Culture has been described as "the personality of the company". That can be refined a bit as the aggregate personality of the employees and executives that make up the company. *Culture* is a compelling concept, yet one that needs practical handles to discover its true value and make it an executable strategy for the company. DATA can be used to map the cultural topology of the company. In effect, an inventory of the personality traits and cognitive abilities of the employees and executives is taken. In any company of size, there will be multiple *cultures*. The IT team will generally have a distinctly different *culture* from the sales team. DATA makes these differences clear and measurable. The company may express a *culture* of values. DATA makes it possible to execute those values using the various behavioral strengths within each internal *culture*. (The next book in the series, *Managing With the Lights On*, will explain this in detail.)

What if I have to hire the candidate regardless of fit?

A chain of supply houses used DATA in all of their hiring. Almost all of the stores were located in larger cities, but there was one in a small town on the coast. The stores in the cities typically had a hundred or more applications for every job. They did the screening with DATA and then used it to select the best candidates, always ones that were strong matches for the jobs. One day the store on the coast called with a strange request, "This candidate was almost screened out. In fact, they are barely acceptable based on the DATA. Is it okay for me to hire them anyway?" The obvious question was, "Why would you want to if they are not really what you need?" The answer was "This is the only person to answer my ad in the last three months." In that situation, he needed to hire the only candidate at the door. In that situation, the DATA is even more important. It tells what is missing and what particular challenges are going to occur with that candidate. With that knowledge, it is possible to prepare additional support in those areas.

Another example of that came when working with a chain of restaurants. None had been fully staffed for most of the year, so the idea of screening out any candidates was not welcome. This restaurant chain focused its marketing on being exceptionally friendly and welcoming. This was stressed in the interviews, but most applicants knew that and were wearing their best smiles for the occasion. The DATA showed which candidates could really be warm and friendly for an entire shift, and which ones might start that way, but would not be able to maintain the smiles. When the managers understood this, they pointed out that the solution was to use the non-smilers on the big tables and the smilers on the two and four tops. Couples and small parties appreciate the friendliness. Large parties are busy with each other and are only interested in the food. Hiring with DATA does not mean that the business always has perfect employees in every position. It means that there will be no Bad Hires, and the candidates that are hired can be positioned to optimize their strengths.

LEGAL ISSUES

Strengthening Non-Discriminatory Hiring Practices

There are many misunderstandings regarding the legal use of testing and assessments in the business world. Certainly there is a maze of federal and state regulations and guidelines that can easily intimidate the average business person. The media has all too often publicized some rather dramatic misuses of testing, creating the impression that is almost a certain recipe for disaster. It is reminiscent of a childhood memory of pleading for a BB gun for a birthday present, and being told that a BB gun would shoot out my eye, my friend's eye, and even the eyes of total strangers. Both of these are fantastic exaggerations of a real, but manageable concern.

The reality is that the proper and consistent use of quality testing and assessment systems can dramatically strengthen a company's legal position. Job-related testing and assessments are essentially the only way to document objective and non-discriminatory hiring practices. In the selection process, the area most susceptible to bias or discrimination is the interviewing. Each interviewer brings conscious and unconscious bias into the interview. They may control it, but it is difficult to document that. Only the testing components are purely objective and can demonstrate their pure objectivity. Skills testing may or may not be measurable depending on the job. Only the hard-wired cognitive abilities and personality traits necessary for any critical job behaviors are completely objective. As Hogan (1990) correctly points out, "bias is a social component of the decision making process, not a feature of the test results; therefore a primary advantage of test use is that tests, unlike interviewers, are incapable of being prejudiced by the applicant's race, gender, ethnicity, national origin, religion, age, or disability."

While this book is principally addressed to employers, it must be remembered that there are always two losers when an employee does not fit the job for which they were hired. The company loses the time, energy and money spent on recruiting, training and coaching, and of course, there is the loss of performance results. Equally important is the employee's loss of time and energy that has been invested in the wrong opportunity. That part of their life cannot be replaced. The information provided by DATA can help each party arrive at the best decision. Every legal guideline and regulation supports that purpose. If fact, *it is inconsistent with the spirit of EEOC and ADA legislation to hire a person for whom the probability of reasonable success in the job is limited.*

Under the Uniform Guidelines on Employee Selection Procedures (1994), a selection process must provide fair and equal employment opportunities to all applicants. Testing may be used:

1) To group applicants in accordance with the likelihood of their successful performance.

2) To group applicants in accordance with the likelihood of their unsuccessful performance.

3) To rank applicants, selecting those with the highest scores for employment.

Armed with knowledge and reasonable awareness, any business can take advantage of the power of assessments and testing information, and at the same time, strengthen its legal compliance.

BACKGROUND CHECKS & SPECIAL TESTING – DRUG, HONESTY, SKILLS TESTING & MORE

Certain types of jobs require specialized tests and screening for unacceptable behaviors. Whenever the job puts the employee into situations that can create legal exposures for the company, it is important to include specialized screening elements into the selection process. For example, if the employee will be driving a company vehicle or if the employee will be performing their job within the homes of customers, an incident may be cause for legal actions against the company. In court, the company will then be asked if there were any measures they could have taken that might have prevented the incident. Failure to use such measures may be judged to be negligent hiring practices.

The use of these screening tools does come with a cost, not only in dollars. There is a certain negativity that is associated with them, as they literally do look for negative facts about the job candidates. Candidates know that and it can affect their willingness to apply for such jobs in companies that use these tools. Overall, that is a good thing. Companies that openly state that all job candidates will be drug tested have found that this act alone kept most drug users from even applying. To a lesser extent, background checks and honesty tests have similar effects. The cost of these types of tests or services can be much greater than that of BestWork DATA. The unlimited license makes it efficient to first screen out those candidates who are poor fits to the job before spending additional money. A basic rule of designing a screening and selection process is to use the most accurate and least expensive method first. BestWork DATA is ideal for that.

A Bit of Caution

Background Checks

Background checks are essential for any responsible position. The range of exaggerations, fabrications, omissions and outright lies that are presented in some resumés and interviews is astonishing. One client who was the president of a rather small company was excited when he received a remarkable resumé from a gentleman applying for a mid-level executive position. The applicant claimed to have an MBA from Harvard and senior level experience at a Fortune 50 company. A skeptical friend asked, "If that is true, why would he apply to work for you?" Of course, the background check revealed the lies.

Not all resumés feature such whoppers; however, recent studies found that almost 80% of all resumés contained some form of misrepresentation or stretches of the truth. It is important to verify education, training certifications and other key points. It is essential for some jobs to avoid applicants with criminal records, although many jobs can be fresh starts for those who have served out their time.

All background checking companies get their information from the same sources. The ease of accessing those sources varies greatly from state to state and even within the states. Some companies have advantages in some areas and they can respond more quickly in those cases. Shop for a company that understands your needs and which can work most effectively with you.

Special Types of Testing

Drug Testing

Applicants for any job that involves working with or around machinery or vehicles should be drug tested. Simply posting the fact that all applicants will be drug tested will eliminate many undesirable candidates who will not even apply. There are many methodologies for drug testing and these are continually changing. There are also a wide range of drugs that can affect safety and job performance. Explore your options with several firms to find the one that best suits your needs.

Alcohol Misuse

Most drug testing companies also have programs for controlling the misuse of alcohol in the workplace. These are usually quite simple and inexpensive, and they should be a part of any selection process for jobs that have a safety issue.

Integrity Testing & More

Integrity testing and honesty testing are part of a family of tests that focus on counterproductive workplace behaviors. These may include employee theft, sexual harassment, misuse of computers, drug use, alcohol use, violence in the workplace, bribery and others. These are all serious problems in business and anything that can minimize their impact is welcome; however, it is important to understand the limitations of these tools. In the United States, the format for such tests must be direct admissions questions. A typical example is "In my previous jobs, I have stolen: a) More than $100 of money and merchandise, b) Less than $100 of money and merchandise or c) Nothing." Similar questions can be directed at drug use or any of the other issues mentioned above. These tests rely on the fact that human beings tend to justify their own behavior. Thieves want to believe that all people steal. Drug users want to believe that all people use drugs. Therefore, with those beliefs, they believe that saying they stole nothing would be seen as a lie, so they admit to a lesser level of theft or drug use or whatever. Of course, this is not true of everyone and certainly not true with all thieves or drug users. Depending upon the population of applicants, these types of tests will screen out about 20% of the problem candidates through their admissions. While that may not seem like much, in the retail business, the average amount of a single employee's theft is almost $2,000. Screening out even one such employee is worthwhile.

These tools have traditionally been focused more on hourly workers. In recent years, there has been a rise in executive or white collar crime with the average incident being $175,000. New technology is being developed to address this problem with more sophisticated tools.

Gamification

A hot topic today is gamification. This involves engaging candidates with gaming formats which translate the candidates' game decisions into characteristics that are important to a particular position. While such exercises are definitely fun and exciting, it is generally more expensive producing information that is less specific than BestWork DATA. The experience is an interesting event, but the applications into the business processes of the company are limited. Gamification is much more effective as a motivational tool.

Skills Testing

If a job requires a certain skill, such as software programming or being able to use certain software programs, it is essential to test the candidate's level of skill. There are many online services that provide tools for this.

REFERENCES – GIVING & RECEIVING

The perfect reference is the one you get from your close friend who is heavily invested in the success of your company and who has first-hand experience working with the individual being referenced, under circumstances nearly identical to those in your situation. Needless to say, most references fall somewhat short of those criteria. Nonetheless, it is a prudent practice to request references and to follow up with them when they are given. Most positive comments, however, should be taken with the proverbial grain of salt, and the reasoning for this will be clear after reading the next paragraph on giving references.

When you are asked for references, limit your response to when that person was first employed and when they left your employment. You should not volunteer any comments on their performance, either positive or negative. If asked if you would hire them again, confine your answer to something noncommittal, such as "It would depend upon the circumstances at the time." Your attorney will be happy if you follow these guidelines.

DEMONSTRATIONS & INBOX EXERCISES

Some jobs lend themselves to having candidates demonstrate their proficiency with key elements of the job. Such demonstrations should not require any special knowledge or training that a normal candidate would not already have. Inbox exercises are a type of demonstration that involves a candidate working through a series of situations found in a typical business day. The candidate demonstrates their problem-solving ability among other things. While these kinds of things can be beneficial, BestWork DATA delivers more accurate information in a much more efficient way.

VALUES & INTEREST SURVEYS –
LOOKING FOR INTANGIBLES

There are characteristics that can be measured accurately and reliably, such as general reasoning and personality traits. There are other characteristics that cannot be **measured** but a candidate's attitude toward those characteristics can be **surveyed.** A survey can explore a candidate's attitude about values, but it cannot actually **measure** those values. A survey can explore a candidate's interests, but it cannot actually measure those interests. The unreliability of these types of tools should exclude them from contributing to any hiring decisions.

Culture, Oh Culture

Many consultants encourage the use of *cultural surveys*, promoting the belief that companies have a particular *culture*, and to be successful, job candidates should fit into that company's *culture*. This makes sense, at first, until you start trying to define exactly what is meant by *culture*. Joshua Rothman in The New Yorker wrote, "Confusion about culture was just part of the culture this year. People were desperate to know what "culture" meant. It goes without saying that "culture" is a confusing word, this year or any year." Every consultant has their own model of culture along with a survey which takes the opinions and attitudes of the managers and employees and builds them into that model. These exercises can make for interesting discussions, but they lend little practical application to the operations of the enterprise. A more useful definition is that *culture* is essentially the collective personality of the company. That collective personality drives the behaviors of the company, and that is immediately practical. In larger companies, DATA normally reveals several different *cultures*. Using the information from the DATA, it is easy to map those and to understand how they interact with each other's.

Don't Get Emotional

Emotional Intelligence (EQ) is another of the many assessments that offer meaningful information for personal development and insights into others. It does not have the same effectiveness for selection decisions. The concept of EQ is that individuals with a high EQ know themselves and their emotions better than other people. Consequently, when answering EQ assessments, they tend to report accurately. Conversely, individuals with a lower EQ do not know themselves and their emotions as well as other people. Consequently, when answering EQ assessments, they tend to overstate their abilities. For example, 80% of people believe they are among the top 50% of emotionally intelligent people. This kind of distortion can be disastrous when selecting employees.

THE MYTHS AND MISSES OF PROFILING

In the world of assessments, a common sales pitch is an offer to test top performers and then create a *success profile, benchmark* or *template* which can then be used to evaluate job candidates. It is a compelling offer. Who would not want more top performers? It sounds easy. Often, the seller will even create the *profile* for free. Does it sound a little too easy or too good to be true? The trap is that it is just true enough to be dangerously wrong. The purpose of this section is to explain those dangers and to suggest an alternative approach.

These observations are based on 20 years of work as a consultant in the assessment industry. They are based on hundreds of actual client experiences using several of the most sophisticated profiling systems. They include the findings from several research projects whose objective was to discover the most effective methods for creating profiles of top performers.

The Simpler the Job, the Better It Works

The concept of profiling top performers originated with simple jobs based on rote behaviors. The concept is woefully inadequate for today's complex jobs, particularly when knowledgework is involved. Performance depends on a complex array of traits and abilities in the individual. It also depends on the interaction with that individual and the manager and with the facility with which they interact with the other members of the team. A simple percentage match to some template is as likely to misdirect the decision as it is to guide it.

What Is a Top Performer?

The cornerstone of the profiling methodology depends upon the ability of the client to accurately and specifically define who a "top performer" is in their business. In hundreds of cases across the United States, managers were unable to agree on exactly who was a "top performer" and why they fit that description. Salespeople were "tops" for such varied metrics as total revenue, percentage of new sales, highest margins, growth of account revenue, percentage of sales of particular products, greatest number of accounts, fastest growth and even anticipated performance. With managers or other jobs with fuzzier metrics, the puzzle is even more challenging.

How Many Top Performers Does It Take for a Robust Sample?

Even assuming that top performers could be identified, a robust sample that could reasonably be expected to yield reliable results would contain 15 or more individuals. A minimum sample for even acceptable results would be 10 individuals. Since the "top performers" would typically represent the top 20% of the group, that would mean that the overall size of a work group suited to this methodology is 50 or more.

Some Factors Are More Important for Performance Than Others

There may be many factors that contribute to success, but experience with hundreds of positions has shown that in every case, two or three of those factors are critical for even adequate performance. The problem is that none of the existing profiling methodologies have an effective process for accurately weighting those factors. In fact, the assessment product with the most sophisticated weighting system is still prone to glaring mistakes. An example of this is a candidate for a persuasive sales role whose percentage match to the success profile was 92%. A 70% match is considered acceptable; an 80% match would be a strong hiring indication; and a 90% match would be exceptionally good. The candidate was a perfect match in every factor except that of assertiveness, in which they scored in the bottom 20%, indicating an extremely submissive nature. It was an example of a single fatal flaw.

Some Individuals Perform Differently With Different Managers
This is seen over and over again in the world of professional sports. A player with a fairly lackluster record is traded to another team, and the new manager seems to unlock a world of potential in a previously unremarkable performer. The same is true in the business world. Top performers depend upon their own abilities, the direction and support of their manager, the interaction with their team and the resources available to them. The "strong match" for one manager could easily be only "acceptable" to a different manager with a different team. The "strong match" to Manager A could even be a "weak match" with Manager B.

If It Does Not Work That Well, Why Do They Use It?
First of all, it is a sales methodology. Assessment publishers with large distributor organizations promote the profiling of top performers

because it is the most effective sales approach for a non-expert sales force. Most distributors are consultants of some kind, using assessments as an entry point or add-on product for their primary business, or they are generally sales organizations and assessments are simply one of their products. The "Test your best. Create a template. Hire more like your best." is an appealing sales pitch. It does not require any particular expertise or knowledge of psychology or psychometrics (the science of measuring personality and cognitive abilities). A common approach is to offer to a create profile for free. This is usually done with far too few individuals in the sample, and rarely is there sufficient analysis to vet the sample. It is only once the profiling program is in use for a time that the flaws in the concept become all too apparent.

Legal Issues Regarding Hiring With Profiles

Here is where it gets a bit sticky. The very nature of hiring templates that require a certain percentage match to that template as a part of a selection process is that the focus of the hiring decision is centered on that element of the process. A company must be strictly consistent with how that percentage match is applied. If an exception is made for some reason, then it may be difficult to defend the nondiscriminatory nature of the process if it were to be challenged. In fact, any challenge to the process by a candidate that has been excluded will center on the hiring profile. It is that profile which must be defended.

The Biggest Problem with Using Profiling

The inherent flaws of success profiling invariably results in hiring nonperformers along with performers. It is the nonperformers that cost money in terms of lost sales, turnover, management time, training time and customer dissatisfaction. The greatest loss, however, is in not realizing the true potential of people. Good assessments provide a clear picture of the strengths and abilities of people. When those are not masked by superfluous templates or benchmarks, it is possible to recognize how to optimize both human and organizational performance.

COGNATIVE ABILITIES
AND THE MANY KINDS OF SMART

First, the Technical Explanation

There is one basic factor that underlies all technical skills and is essential to all jobs. That is cognitive ability, or intelligence. The importance of intelligence to on-the-job performance has been highlighted by Seligman (1997) who reported that the overwhelming body of research supports the conclusion that "Intelligence matters in all jobs," although how much it matters depends on the nature of the job. By intelligence we mean the speed of thinking, how readily new material is learned and how quickly underlying patterns are recognized and decisions made in response to those patterns. In the development of the BestWork DATA instruments, an early decision was made to include a measure of the participant's cognitive skills, especially in the areas of fluid intelligence, inductive reasoning and general sequential understanding, as well as quantitative understanding. On the basis of both research and professional experience, it was clear that these particular cognitive skills were important to on-the-job success, regardless of the job to be performed.

The Cognitive scale of the BestWork DATA instruments is largely based upon Guildford's Structure of Intellect model in which it is assumed that cognitive ability or intelligence is best understood as a composite of several separate abilities. While it is beyond the scope of this book to present the Guilford model, it seemed clear to us that not all of those abilities have a direct impact upon workplace performance. The research (see Flanagan, Genshaft, & Harrison (1997) for comprehensive review of this literature) and our professional experience led us to select two of nine abilities, Fluid Intelligence/Reasoning and Quantitative Reasoning/Knowledge, for inclusion in the BestWork DATA instruments. The omission of Crystallized Intelligence/Knowledge was a deliberate one. Although we were aware of the important role of crystallized intelligence, including vocabulary, in any comprehensive view of cognitive ability, this was tempered by our desire to make the BestWork DATA instruments as culture-free as possible. While language-based items, of course, were included, items tapping pure crystallized intelligence, i.e., vocabulary, were not. This reduces the cultural bias of the BestWork DATA instruments and eliminates the principal cause of adverse impact.

For the Fluid Reasoning ability, three sub-areas were included:
1. General sequential reasoning (the ability to start with stated rules, premises or conditions and to engage in one or more steps to reach a solution to a problem)
2. Induction (the ability to discover the underlying characteristic, e.g., rule concept, process or trend of class membership that governs a problem or as set of materials)
3. Speed of reasoning (the ability to solve problems quickly)

For the Quantitative Reasoning/Knowledge ability, two sub-areas were included:

1. Quantitative reasoning (the ability to inductively and deductively reason with concepts involving mathematical concepts and properties)

2. Mathematical knowledge (the ability to solve a range of mathematical problems)

These scales combine to present a remarkably robust measure of general reasoning speed, which has long been accepted as a key factor in workplace success in virtually all types of jobs.

Now, What It Means and Why It Is Important...

One of the wonderful effects of using BestWork DATA is how it shatters the old concept of "smart" and "not smart" people. ALL PEOPLE ARE SMART! They are "smart" in different ways. DATA focuses on speed of learning, how quickly a person can acquire new information and how quickly they can process that information. Here is the surprise for most people: faster processing is not necessarily better than slower processing. It all depends upon the job. If a job involves complex procedures that change frequently, a faster speed of learning is definitely desirable. On the other hand, if the procedures are well defined and tend to remain stable, there is little need for a faster learning speed. In fact, with little change and little new information, a person who learns quickly will easily become bored. Fast information processors cannot handle extended routine tasks.

People who learn more slowly can be "geniuses" at routine, finding it satisfying to do that routine task correctly time after time.

An excellent example of this was found in one of the premier professional accounting firms. The managing partners of the audit practice, with MBA's from prestigious business schools, were usually slow information processors clustering around the 30th percentile in speed of learning. Audit are slow processing jobs which demand meticulous processes. No one is seeking a rapid audit...just an accurate one.

In that same firm, the managing partners of the tax division, with similar MBA's, were found around the 70th percentile. Tax regulations changed frequently and each client presented different challenges, requiring a quicker time acquiring the problems and working out solutions.

The fastest information processors were found in the consulting practice. Every client was different, and each one presented a complex array of problems. The consultants had to acquire the information quickly: integrate it into the firm's solution models; and offer a compelling plan for an engagement with the client. All of the consultants therefore were found in the 90th percentile in speed of learning and processing information. They also had the requisite MBA's, but as with the other cases, it was their cognitive abilities that determined in what part of the practice that knowledge could best be used.

Speed of learning comes with speed of communicating. This is one of the most common problems found in companies. Too often, a talented executive with a faster learning speed finds it difficult to communicate with some of their team because of their different speeds of communication. It is important to understand that the faster processor can slow down their communication, but the slower one cannot speed up their ability to capture the message. DATA makes such communication gaps visible, and once they are recognized, it is easy to bridge the gap.

Cognitive abilities also determine the most effective focus of attention to the business operations and planning. Slower processors have an excellent focus on the immediate operations and the problems that require attention right away. Fast processors have the best focus on the future or the strategic issues facing the business. They are less clear about immediate issues. The majority of people fall into the middle of the bell curve, processing information at an average rate of speed. Their focus is on tactical planning and near term developments. Successful businesses need all of these perspectives, although the type of business will determine which are most important.

Cognitive science today enables businesses to recognize how each employee can best contribute to the overall success of the enterprise. The proper use of DATA and other information is invaluable in revealing the amazing value within each person, regardless of their education.

REPORT SAMPLES – *MANAGE ME* AND *MY MANAGER*

Manage Me Report

This report gives the manager or supervisor a quick look at the key performance issues that can occur with this individual. A fire marshall surveys a building and then calls out the areas that are most likely to have a fire. It does not mean there is a fire or that there will be a fire. It means that particular attention should be paid to those areas. In the same way, the *Manage Me* Report is a reminder that all individuals have areas which will cause challenges at some time. These are simply areas that need more attention than others. *Manage Me* is meant to help you step back and look at the employee objectively when there is a problem. Used properly, it can point out the source of the problem quickly and guide you to a positive solution.

Manage Me is an excellent focus for discussions, either on an ongoing basis with regular meetings and coaching, or in conjunction with training or performance reviews. A sample *Manage Me* Report is provided here. Areas of particular note are in BOLD type; these are important ones for communication and feedback over the life cycle of the employee.

> **IMPORTANT NOTE:** This report focuses on potential issues. It does not present a balanced view nor does it present this individual's strengths. Use the other BestWork reports for a clear understanding of the whole person. "No issues" indicates that there are no outstanding concerns in this area.

DETAILS
- No issues

PLANNING
- No issues

TIME MANAGEMENT
- Has adequate time management
- Usually prioritizes effectively
- Can benefit from the use of proven time management tools

SPEED OF LEARNING
- Learns new information quickly
- Needs a continual challenge to avoid becoming bored

COMMUNICATING WITH OTHERS
- **Can sometimes communicate ideas and information too quickly for others to fully understand**
- **Information can also seem incomplete to others**
- **Important to slow down and verify understanding of others**

CALLING OUT PROBLEMS
- **Is reluctant to call out problems**

SENSE OF URGENCY
- Impatient
- Can seem to have frequent crises or emergencies

LISTENING
- No issues

FOLLOWING RULES
- Does not follow rules or procedures
- Important that they know the limits of flexibility

HANDLING CHANGE
- Handles change easily

ASKING FOR HELP
- No issues

ADMITTING WEAKNESSES
- No issues

My Manager Report

The BestWork DATA Experience measures personality traits and cognitive abilities that tend to remain stable over time.

> **IMPORTANT NOTE:** This report is selected from the manager's menu of reports, and it uses the manager's scores for its output.

This report applies those measurements to specific behaviors that are related to working with your manager. Using this information, you can more quickly gain an understanding of how to communicate more effectively and perform your job better under this manager's supervision. Areas of particular note are in BOLD type. This sample report is not intended to be comprehensive but rather it is designed to highlight key points that are most likely to enhance communication and understanding.

MANAGER'S SPEED OF COMMUNICATION
- This manager's explanations can be quick and incomplete; they assume that you see and know the same things as they do.
- It is important to ask questions to clarify your understanding of what they are saying.
- When you present your ideas to them, the ideas must be well thought out but presented clearly and concisely.

MANAGER'S NEED FOR CONTROL
- **This manager has a high need for control.**
- It is important for you to demonstrate knowledge and ability to complete projects successfully in order to be given more responsibility.
- Having a delegation plan makes this easier.

MANAGER'S FEEDBACK TO YOU
- This manager's feedback is direct.
- **The feedback can be too direct at times.**
- It is important for you to hear the underlying message despite what might be considered poor delivery.

MANAGER'S DISCUSSION STYLE
- This manager expects debate or discussions that may challenge their opinion as a means of validating the idea.
- It must be presented in an appropriate and professional manner.
- It is important to note that lack of discussion or challenge is interpreted as agreement.

MANAGER'S LEVEL OF DETAILS & ORGANIZATION
- This manager is not good with details.
- It is important for you to help with organization and details of projects.

MANAGER'S SENSE OF URGENCY
- This manager is relaxed and calm.
- They do not communicate a sense of urgency much of the time.

- **It is important for you to know the specific deadlines so that you can work to meet them.**

MANAGER'S CONSISTENCY
- **This manager can be inconsistent with urgency.**
- They can frequently change direction or priorities.
- It is important for you to clarify your understanding of what the key priorities are so that you can accomplish your goals despite the changes that may be less important and distracting.

MANAGER'S TIME MANAGEMENT
- **This manager has loose time management.**
- Meetings can be late or last longer than scheduled.
- Adapt your schedule as necessary and communicate your own time limits.
- When waiting, use time productively.

MANAGER'S FLEXIBILITY
- This manager is usually open to new ideas.
- They are willing to try different options and adapt to new situations.
- They will make exceptions.

MANAGER'S LISTENING
- This manager is usually a good listener.
- They may not participate in the discussion even though they are listening.
- **It is important for you to ask questions to confirm their understanding of what you are communicating.**

MANAGER'S PROBLEM SOLVING
- This manager is an excellent problem solver.
- They may see alternative solutions that are not seen by others.

MANAGER'S FOCUS OF ATTENTION
- This manager tends to focus more on strategic issues and where the company is going.

- They may talk more about their vision of the future and may have fewer details about what to do in the present.

MANAGER'S DECISION-MAKING
- **This manager usually makes decisions quickly.**
- It is important to help them have necessary information related to those decisions.

MANAGER'S EMOTIONS
- This manager does not show enthusiasm or emotions outwardly.
- **Do not assume something is wrong because they do not appear happy at times.**

MANAGER'S HANDLING OF STRESS
- This manager can handle high levels of stress.
- They may not recognize when you need to take a break.
- **It is important for you to communicate that need, when necessary.**

MANAGER'S COMPETITIVENESS
- This manager looks for win-win situations and team collaboration to achieve common goals.
- They expect to see you work hard for the team's success and appreciate your efforts.

MANAGER'S AVILABILITY
- This manager is usually quite available.
- They are open to interruptions when level of importance and urgency warrants it.
- They tend to interrupt you whenever needed.

MANAGER'S SESITIVITY TO MORALE
- This manager may not be aware of morale issues with employees.
- It is important for you to communicate difficult situations to them and not wait for them to ask you.

SUMMING UP

It is my goal that this book will disrupt your old thinking about job performance and hiring. I want it to open up a world of possibilities that can transform your company or simply help you to understand your own job and how it matches up with your hard-wired strengths and abilities. BestWork DATA was not born in academics or from a research project. It was designed from the practical and pragmatic world of entrepreneurial business. It has been proven in major companies. It does not hype massive meta-analyses that mean nothing to the average businessperson. It does not have legions of salespeople pushing outdated instruments using outdated methodologies. It is based on sound science and common sense. Anyone can understand the information without consultants or experts. It requires no special training. The information is clear. It simply works. It has spread to larger enterprises because it simply works.

BestWork DATA is a disruptive innovation that can change your world. Be my guest and give it a try as my 'thank you' for purchasing this book. See the **BestWork DATA Free Pilot Program** at the end of the book.

ABOUT THE AUTHOR

Chuck Russell is a thought leader in the business applications of predictive DATA that measure how people think, learn and behave. His first book, *Right Person-Right Job, Guess or Know*, showed how the information provided by the latest generation of assessment technology shattered the traditional paradigms of management, hiring and training. After years of being the national expert for several major instruments, Chuck recognized that the majority of businesses would never have the benefits of these tools as long as their use depended on experts and specialized knowledge. Over the last ten years, he has developed a series of disruptive innovations within the assessment industry. The result is BestWork DATA, an easy-to-use system that virtually eliminates bad hires and at the same time, provides specific talent management information throughout the lifecycle of employees. Using this DATA, early adopters have experienced results that are not just better, but are game changing within their industries. DATA is making true human capital management possible, and at the same time, powering analytics of human performance that are transforming many traditional business concepts.

Chuck's mission is to touch the lives of hundreds of millions of people, so that they see themselves through their strengths and not their weaknesses, and so that they better understand others.

Chuck has a degree in Economics from Spring Hill College, and is a member of Mensa. He is an excellent tennis player and also owns golf clubs. His wonderful wife, Lauretta, teaches the Suzuki piano method in her studio. Chuck's favorite and most important job is being the Dad for his son and daughter. Away from the business world, Chuck is a screenwriter and director, currently working on a feature length movie.

For information on booking Chuck for a speaking engagement, visit www.chucksthoughts.com.

BIBLIOGRAPHY

Bartram, David (1990). **Measuring Differences Between People**, England: Nfer-Nelson.

Bennett, Nathan & Russell, Chuck (2014). **Big Data and Talent Management: Using Hard Data to Make the Soft Stuff Easy**, Business Horizons.

Blanchard, Ken & Johnson, Spencer (1986). **The One Minute Manager**, William Morrow & Company.

Bosworth, Michael (1995). **Solution Selling**, McGraw Hill.

Buckingham, Marcus & Clifton, Donald (2001). **Now, Discover Your Strengths**, The Free Press.

Bureau of National Affairs, Inc. (1990). **Uniform Guidelines on Employment Selection Procedures**.

Buros Institute (1993-1999). **The Mental Measurements Yearbooks**, University of Nebraska.

Christensen, Clayton (1997). **The Innovator's Dilemma**, HarperBusiness.

Collins, Jim (2001). **Good To Great**, HarperCollins.

Dixon, Matthew & Adamson, Brent (2011). **The Challenger Sale**, Penguin Books.

Duston, Robert L. (1992). **The Effect of the ADA on Employee Selection Procedures**, University Publications of America.

Flanagan, D. P., Genshaft, J. L. & Harrison, P. L. (Eds.) (1992). **Contemporary Intellectual Assessment: Theories, Tests and Issues,** The Guilford Press.

Gardner, Howard (1992). **Frames of Mind**, New York: Doubleday.

Gardner, Howard (1993). **Multiple Intelligences**, Basic Books.

Greenberg, Herbert & Greenberg, Jeane (1980). **Job-Matching for Better Sales Performance,** *Harvard Business Review.*

Hall, Calvin & Lindsey, Gardner (1978). **Theories of Personality**, John Wiley & Sons.

Hedges, Krisi. (May, 2015). **Why Job Interviews Are Like Flipping A Coin,** *Forbes.*

Howard, Pierce J. (1994). **The Owner's Manual for the Brain**, Leornian Press.

Jaques & Cason (1994). **Human Capability**, Cason Hall & Co.

Jaques, Elliott (2002). **The Life and Behavior of Living Organisms**, Praeger.

Johnson, Spencer (1998). **Who Moved My Cheese**, G.P. Putnam's Sons.

Keyser, D.J. & Sweetland, R.C. (1984-1988), **Test Critiques (Vols. I-VII).** Texas: Pro-Ed.

Kline, Paul (1991). **Intelligence: The Psychometric View.** London, Routledge.

Kline, Paul (1992). **Psychometric Testing in Personnel Selection & Appraisal**, Corner Publications Ltd.

Kline, Paul (1993). **The Handbook of Psychological Testing**. London: Routledge.

Lanyon, Richard & Goodstein, Leonard (1997). **Personality Assessment**, John Wiley & Sons.

Leadership IQ Company, Global Talent Management Survey, 2012.

McCrae, Robert R. & Costa, Paul T. (1987). **Validation of the Five-Factor Model of Personality Across Instruments and Observers,** *Journal of Personality and Social Psychology,* Vol. 52, No. 1.

O'Grady, Jenn & Visocky, Ken (2008). **The Information Design Handbook**, How Books.

Rackham, Neil (1988). **Spin Selling**, McGraw Hill.

Rothman, Joshua (December, 2014). **The Meaning of "Culture"**, *The New Yorker.*

Russell, Chuck (1996). **Right Person - Right Job, Guess or Know,** Johnson & James.

Schwartz, Barry (2004). **The Paradox of Choice**, Harper Perennial.

Seligman, Martin. (2002) **Authentic Happiness,** The Free Press.

Walsh, Bruce & Betz, Nancy (2001). **Tests and Assessment**, Prentice Hall.

Westgaard, Odin (1999). **Tests That Work**, Jossey-Bass.

Zemke, Ron (April, 1992). **Second Thoughts About the MBTI,** *Training,* Vol. 29, No. 4.

BESTWORK DATA FREE PILOT PROGRAM

The first step is easy and free. Included in your purchase of this book is the ability to identify the strengths and talents of three individuals. Simply go to www.bestworkdata.com/nobadhires and register with the author. You can also elect to receive notices of Chuck's podcasts, blogs and future books.

Once you have registered, you will be given a unique link which will enable three people to complete the BestWork DATA experience. When that has been done, you will have access to a menu of several different reports. You are welcome to try any or all of the reports in the menu with your participants. BestWork DATA has hundreds of reports within its system, covering virtually any type of job. This experience will enable you to see how BestWork DATA can help you eliminate **Bad Hires**.

Your selection of BestWork DATA reports includes:
- *Sales Quick Screen Chart*
- *Sales Strengths Chart*
- *Persuasive Sales Job Report*
- *Management Job Report*
- *Project Manager Job Report*
- *Financial/Admin/IT Job Report*

- *Working with Me Report*
- *Communication Keys*

Some suggestions:
- Choose one or two of the people who work closely with you. Read each other's *Working with Me Report.*
- If you have a sales person struggling, check the *Persuasive Sales Job Report* to see what their challenges may be.
- Share *Communication Keys* with a coworker.

BestWork DATA Reports

The BestWork DATA system contains hundreds of reports, each one written for a specific decision point in the operation of a business. While this book focuses on talent acquisition, BestWork DATA programs are available for performance management, talent development, team engineering, pre-training analytics, leadership inventories, sales team optimization and many more. Industry-specific programs are available, which address the key issues within that industry and use the terminology of the industry. These include call centers, fast-casual restaurants, banking, insurance, healthcare, manufacturing, education, real estate, consulting and many more.

AUTHOR'S NOTE: The discovery that all human beings have hard-wired personality traits and cognitive abilities is empowering. This means that you have wonderful strengths that never go away. They are always there for you to use.

The more specifically you understand these strengths, the more able you are to put yourself into positions in which your strengths give you an advantage. BestWork DATA is not simply another product. It is a completely different way of viewing yourself and others in an incredibly positive way. It is a realization that goes far beyond the business world, touching every aspect of your life.

Chuck Russell

Made in the USA
Middletown, DE
23 December 2019

81857131R00156